# REMEMBERING

# FORGETTING

To Fiona
Speak truth to power
Keep the faith

*Other titles in 2001 from Otford Press*


*To Tibet with a box brownie; Gina Behrens*
*God on Trial; Robert Colquhoun*
*Moving Mountains: Communities confront Mining and Globalisation; James Goodwin (Ed)*
*Pillars of Fear; Bruce Haigh*
*The Great Australian Blight; Bruce Haigh*
*A guide to Australian WWI battlefields in France and Belgium; Bruce Haigh*
*Stirrings of Nationalism in East Timor, FRETILIN 1974-78; Helen Hill*
*The Timid and the Brave; Liz Howells*
*Media-crity; Jefferson Lee*
*GodZone; J.R. McNamara*
*One Man in his Time; Hans Post*
*Kiwis, Bludgers and Saints; Robert Pyper*
*Gold Dust, Bull Dust; Robert Pyper*
*The Visa; Wes Russell*
*Telling Lies for Little Johnnie; Wayne Sievers*
*West Papua: The Campaign for Justice; Keith Suter*
*With a Dzong in my Heart; Lansell Taudevin*
*The Aid Virus; Lansell Taudevin*
*Shooting the Messenger; Lansell Taudevin*
*East Timor: Making Amends? Lansell Taudevin and Jefferson Lee (Eds)*
*Tetun – English, English –Tetun Dictionary; Teresa Ward (Ed)*


*Visit our web site: www.otfordpress.com.au*

# REMEMBERING FORGETTING

## A Journey of Non-violent Resistance to the War in East Timor

# CIARON O'REILLY

Contemporary Otford
**Otford Press**
**Otford (Sydney), Kula Lumpur and Dili**

# The Contemporary Otford Series

*Published by:*
Otford Press,
49 Station Rd,
Otford, NSW 2508
e-mail: otfordpress@bigpond.com
web site: www.otfordpress.com .au
ABN 48 674 844 898

National Library of Australia
Catalogue-in-Publication entry:
O'Reilly, Ciaron
Remembering Forgetting

Includes index.
ISBN 1 876928 30 1
1. Activism, 2 Politics, 3. East Timor, 4. Asia, I. Title. (Series Otford Contemporary (Otford Press))

Cover design by Malaya Wilmott
Otford Press Logo by Malaya Wilmott
Printed by Printing Creations, Sydney

# Acknowledgements

*Many thanks to some fine Brisbane folks who have 'hung in', 'shown up' and confronted power since the 1970's: Lachlan Hurse, Sue Monk, Gary McLennan, Chris Anderson and Chris Maver.*

*Also thanks to some more recent compañeros: Treena Lenthall, Rachel Harrison, Damien LeGoullon and the Christian Brothers.*

*All these good folks have helped to get this reflection produced and launched.*

*Many thanks to all the East Timorese, Scousers and others who have shared the journey, court scenes and jail cells.*

*We're nearly home, but not quite yet.....*

'Just as it used to be said that the Devil had all the good tunes, so the modern state has a monopoly on the tools and use of violence. Whether responding to George W Bush's Star Wars or John Prescott's fist, we cannot waste time confronting them on their own terms: what is possible for the Zapatistas is suicide for the Scousers. In this context, the Catholic Worker remains a shining example of radical pacifism and the possibility of real change. Ten cheers for them, and for Ciaron O'Reilly's new book.'

*Alex Cox*

*Alex Cox, English film director whose credits include 'Sid and Nancy', 'Repo Man', and 'Walker'. He is presently working on a film about Keith Moon of 'The Who'.*

# Contents

# Foreward

## Daniel Berrigan

Unpretentious, sturdy, bracing; also irrepressible, a spontaneous combustion of community and solidarity. But also more solemn implications; classical, biblical, deeply traditional. A worthy commentary on the Acts of The Apostles, following to the letter its rhythms, from upper room, prayer and liturgy, to the streets and confrontation with the powers. Such are reminders as I ponder Ciaron's text, labours of love wafting him afar, from Australia to East Timor to England (he might have added the US as well, where he and I first met, happily for me).

How can his story not be deeply serious? Lives and deaths, in huge numbers are at stake, under the collusion of awesome principalities - systems greedy and foolish and armed tooth and claw against the innocent and unarmed; (or in the principled faith of Ciaron and his companeros - with all due deliberation - the disarmed).

My brother Philip, presently a ward of Mr. Bush's Justice Warren, has remarked on a compliment that often comes his way. In his estimate it misses the mark.

He is, so falls the praise, a 'man of singular courage'. No, he avers, don't speak of courage. Speak rather of faith.

I ponder that quite serious distinction. I think Philip sees the matter somewhat like this; courage is a kind of set-jaw attainment. You heave and heave, putting shoulder against the invisible wall of fear, routine, family, ego, chic despair, the ho-hum culture of the self damned. And in time the wall falls to a rubble. You walk.

Faith is something else again. It's a gift, albeit a gift that demands, in the inelegant phrase, being worked on. But a gift nonetheless, with all the implications of a 'first move' on the part of Someone Else, of probable undeservedness on the part of you, me, anyone.

The closest analogy I think is falling in love; it happens, it comes home like a clap of lightning, for the moment, the epiphany, it stops the breath. None of us can claim to deserve it, most of us pause at times to wonder at it. Me, greatly loved?

Yes. The Gift, infinitely to be honoured, esteemed, cozened with a Capital Letter.

Anyway, the word occurred to me; faith, as I followed Ciaron across seas and continents, this restless nimble spirit, this (literally and metaphorically) Gifted one of our torrid, tormented era.

The dreadlocks, the elegance, the hefty frame, the rhetoric of scorn and celebration, the sheer brazen unstoppable vision embodied; Ciaron talking the talk (the right talk, the rare and endangered truth), Ciaron walking the walk (a trail of tears to be sure, but a joyous dance as well).

He's been there, done that; he's on pilgrimage with those who pay up. He knows there's no free trip, there's a toll gate along every highway.

Stand somewhere, walk there, sit there, refuse there, sing there, get dragged away there. Pay up, or join the inhumans.

God help us and God be thanked. And hey there, Ciaron - a kiss of the hand to you.

The Irishman, he's living (count them), two times a life!

Daniel

# Meeting Ciaron O'Reilly

## Max Stahl

I shall never forget the wet, the cold, the grey light, around the British Aerospace factory near Preston on the day that I first saw Ciaron in action. I was recently back from East Timor. The mention of this small island occupied for 20 years by Indonesia instantly brought me back to the tension there. It was palpable on every village face, suffocating, stamping even on your thoughts. The might of Indonesia's military machine flattened the people of that tiny nation invaded, slaughtered and occupied in violation of every international and moral law. In graphic contrast to strategic Kuwait, the world pushed East Timor down the memory hole. My task as a film maker was to show the life which survived there, vibrant, but hidden in the cracks.

And then, suddenly, it seemed to me, a few plane hours away, I was thrown into the focused mayhem of Ciaron O'Reilly's kind of army. A priest, two Japanese Buddhist monks patting their flat drums, a schoolteacher, a couple of young civil servants, several mums, casual workers, unemployed local people, each one seemingly a different dynamo, gathered from here and there. Some were from the small congregation of a run down Catholic church in Liverpool, odd ones veterans of the Green protest movement, or peace campaigns against atomic installations in the USA or habitat destruction in Poland or Sweden (yes Sweden!).

They were picketing the guarded gates of the BAe factory because multi-million pound military planes were produced there for shipment to Indonesia and potential use in 8,000 miles away in East Timor.

For the three or four young Timorese among them, this was as bizarre a change as their sudden escape to freedom in a red cross van which plucked them from the ring of steel placed around the US embassy in Jakarta which they had occupied in protest at the US supported occupation of their country.

For me it was an education. Here were ordinary, powerless people making connections, taking ownership of the big questions, doing the impossible. Here ordinary moral values were confronting big military business, reclaiming the abstract political and technical space in which weapons of death are manufactured and traded in the modern world. And these campaigners had put on no airs for the occasion. They sang, and prayed and stood politely, remembering the names of the dead I had filmed in East Timor, putting questions politely but directly on their placards, as if it were the normal thing to do. And at the very heart of this extraordinarily joyful, damp occasion on a wet, cold Lancashire factory gate was a tall, eloquent Australian with long hair, who clearly knew exactly what to do.

It was a concept I, as a hardboiled journo or undercover filmmaker, had a hard time getting my head around. All my instincts rebelled against it. Faced with a steamroller, I knew what to do: find a drain, a hole in the road, get out of the way! Change your place, your face, your name! (I had done all of these in pursuit of the hidden story). Here was a man who stood in the middle of a road with like-minded friends and sang, or prayed out loud, holding hands, naming and renaming the crimes being committed so far away with the machines being made here! I tried to imagine what effect this could have on the Timor I had just visited, and could not.

Six years later however, East Timor is free. The army of occupation has gone, the multiple spies hired in every village and family have dissipated. The problems the new nation faces are many but more familiar: recovery, unemployment, petty crime.

And the people who stood outside the factory gates, and the women who entered the British Aerospace factory and disabled a Hawk airplane in Lancashire are gratefully remembered by many in East Timor, not merely because they helped to raise the profile of their struggle, challenged the politicians far away when no one wanted to know, but because they established that the power of a moral idea crosses borders and distance and ordinary people have power when they act in solidarity. This in the end was the force that routed the men of guns in East Timor.

Ciaron O'Reilly made me think in a way few other people I have ever met made me think. He connected words and thoughts with actions. He offered a method and a habit of challenging the machines of brutal oppression cloaked in a numbing mist of obfuscating abstractions by applied moral dialogue. And he did so directly, without the aid of institutions, learned qualifications, the licensed criticism which rearranges the furniture on the deck of the ocean liners which continue to plough through the weak and vulnerable, plough under the victims we demonise or seek to forget in East Timor and so many other places.

His courage took on targets, big and small, near and far, regardless of power and wealth, by acting on the principles most of us believe we live by. He had been in prison in America, arrested countless times. He had given up the idea of having money, which would all go to paying huge fines, put aside any thoughts of a career, or even a home, in order to build a community capable of empowering the words of religion that people of his age and mine had encased in ceremony and castrated in daily life.

His crusade was not personal. It was shared. There were others. They were not led by Ciaron. They did this on their own initiative. But he played a key role in bedding in the initiative they showed, giving it form and meaning, connecting it with the experience he had learned elsewhere, other non-violent battlegrounds where protest challenges death machines and questions the logic of armies and fighting.

I cannot say that I am quite convinced. Perhaps the debilitating logic of war and deterrent has an iron grip on me. Stepping out of it can be naïve, destabilizing, even dangerous.

But I know that not stepping out of it is the slow death of values.

Ciaron O'Reilly is a peace crusader. The movement he shares and champions so fearlessly lays a moral and intellectual challenge down for all of us who seek to understand conflict. Jerusalem today is certainly not the beacon of peace and life of which violent Crusaders once dreamed. But if there is a New Jerusalem, where the end is not separated from the means, where peace in Iraq or East Timor is not fought for with fighter planes, but claimed by brave and peaceful insistence, then Ciaron O'Reilly is laying the road that might lead there.

He is not merely talking, or even filming. He is there on the front line, building the road. He and so many others in the peace movement are challenging the rest of us by example.

East Timor, I remember hearing, had no chance whatsoever of gaining its freedom. All the realists agreed, up to 1999, when the pressure of action in small doses around the world found a weak spot in the collapse of the thirty-five year rule of Indonesia's military dictator Soeharto, and his nominated successor found that the erstwhile international supporters melted away in his hour of need, because even cynical politicians do not want to be associated with the continuing occupation of East Timor.

It is a fact that sometimes faith moves mountains.

Top: Disarmed British Aerospace Hawk with Indonesian markings
Bottom: Peace campaigners Andrea Needham, Angela Zelter,
Lotta Kronlid and Joanna Wilson outside Liverpool
Crown Court after being cleared of smashing the Hawk Jet

# Hawk jet protesters win top peace prize

By GRAHAM READFEARN

ANGER today greeted the decision to give an international peace prize to four protesters cleared by a jury after causing £1.5 million worth of damage to a British Aerospace jet.

Andrea Needham, Joanna Wilson and Lotta Kronlid freely admitted they broke into the BAe Warton base and attacked a Hawk jet with hammers in January last year.

But along with Angela Zelter, who was found not guilty of conspiring to damage, they are to receive a prestigious medal from The International Peace Bureau in a European Parliament ceremony next week.

Fylde councillors and union representatives branded the decision a disgrace and an insult.

Coun Kiran Mulholland said: "To give them any sort of honour is atrocious. I deplore their actions of damaging private property.

"The analogy is the IRA. They may have an argument but the answer is not to blow people up but to address it through the system. I think without any doubt this is condoning terrorism."

Coun Michael Gilbert said most of his comments would be "unprintable", adding: "When quite blatant law breakers are given an award it is just asking for trouble."

Frank Coulton, chairman of the MFS engineering union at Warton, said: "Are we encouraging people that the way to get your own way is to break the law?

"I am sure the majority of the workers would be insulted by this award."

Today British Aerospace, which was shocked when the women were acquitted on charges of criminal damage last July, refused to comment on the award.

## Respect

A spokesman said: "We have always said that while we respect everyone's right to peaceful protest we also have the right to continue with our lawful business.

"As was pointed out in Parliament, there is no evidence that

the Hawk jets are being used as the protesters have claimed against the civilian population in East Timor. We do not want to make a comment about the peace prize at this stage."

Lancaster and Wyre Prospective Parliamentary candidate and former fighter pilot Keith Mans said that while he supported the right to peaceful protest, he thought the award of the prize to the four women would shock many local people.

He said : "I am disappointed that this group, that has a long history, did not feel that there were other more worthwhile causes for the award.

"It may send the wrong message to people that if they damage property in this way it could lead to similar peace awards."

Joanna Wilson, speaking from

Brussels, said today: "We hope that the International Peace Bureau's decision to recognise the legitimacy and importance of our action will send a message to both the British Government and European Parliament that this lethal trade must stop now."

The Nobel Prize winning International Peace Bureau, based in Geneva, will present the women with the Sean MacBride Peace Prize – a non-monetary award named after the respected Irish journalist, lawyer and politician.

Colin Archer, secretary general of the IPB, said of the criticism: "These women have been upholding the law not breaking it. Peace needs people to take bold actions."

■ More protesters in court. Page 13.

Rui Zimenes, survivor of detention and torture by the
Indonesian military leads walk to BAe Warton

Steven Hancock and the author awaiting sentencing at the
High Court London

Rehearsing human ladder approach to clearing BAe's fence,
Liverpool

Author stages die-in blocking entry to military HQ in protest
at the training of Indonesian troops

Beginning the 45 mile peace walk from Liverpool Crown Court to BAe Warton on the anniversary of the Ploughshare acquittal

Author arrested at the Department of Trade and Industry for
resisting arms sales to Indonesia

# Prologue

## Gary MacLennan

When Ciaron asked me to contribute a prologue to this book, I said 'yes' immediately. After all I have known him as a good friend and fellow activist for over twenty years and his father, Garrett, is one of the people I admire most in this world. Yet, for all that I often boast of being able to write 2000 words on anything, I found this task a difficult one. In truth, reading through these pages has proved to be a deeply confronting experience. I would like, if I may, to face up honestly to what caused me such difficulty.

To begin with there is the stumbling block of Ciaron's faith. This book is the testimony of a deeply spiritual and profoundly religious man. His many actions frequently centre on a symbolic act. Always he turns to prayer and meditation. The prayers and symbols themselves are drawn largely from the Roman Catholic Church. Thus there is much talk of sharing bread and wine.

I would like it to be clear here that my objections or negative reactions are not drawn from the tradition of rationalist opposition to Christian obscurantism. I am far too Irish for that. No. The problem is that Ciaron and I share the same religious background. I too was born into the Catholic Church, but I now regard that same church as nothing less than a monstrous evil.

1

Moreover, leaving it, for me, was **the** moment of liberation of my lifetime, a moment that I will never betray.

Ciaron is of course aware of the history of Catholicism. He is aware too of the silences and compromises that the Australian Catholic hierarchy perpetrated in the face of genocide in East Timor. As with that other great moral test of the 20th century, the genocide of the Jewish people, the Catholic Church was tested over East Timor and it was found wanting. Here Ciaron quotes Albert Camus to great effect.

'For a long time during those frightful years (pre-WWII) I waited for a great voice to speak up (in the Church). I, an unbeliever? Precisely, for I knew that the spirit would be lost if it did not offer a cry of condemnation when faced with force. What the world expects of Christians is that Christians should speak out loud and clear. That they should get away from abstraction and confront the bloodstained face history has taken on today. The grouping that we need is a grouping of people resolved to speak out clearly and pay up personally.' (Albert Camus)

It must be said that we now know that the Church was not simply silent in the face of the rise of Nazism. It was, rather, a willing partner. Thus the Pope instructed the Catholic Party in the German Parliament to vote for Hitler's accession to power.

As for the case of East Timor, despite their almost certain knowledge of the massacre of thousands of Catholics, the Australian Catholic bishops remained resolutely silent. No doubt their compromise was justified to themselves in the name of preventing a greater tragedy for Catholics elsewhere in Indonesia. Perhaps their Holinesses told themselves there was nothing they could do. The truth is otherwise of course.

East Timor was invaded in 1975, and all the powerful connived at that invasion. The invading army did what invading armies always do. They raped and murdered. The same army had massacred over two million Communists a mere nine years before in the mainland of Indonesia. In the eyes of the Western powers, their anti-communist credentials were impeccable. By the time they had finished in East Timor, their victims numbered in excess of a quarter of a million.

How was such an evil possible? The answer lies as always in the specificities of the political conjuncture. Vietnam had just fallen to the Communist Viet Cong and the West was hungry for revenge. The talk of Marxism in East Timor, and it was never more than talk, was all that it took. Presidents and Prime Ministers agreed to the invasion and the subsequent sowing of the killing fields. They said 'yes' to power and evil and for that may they all rot in eternal damnation.

That solemn curse brings me to the other source of my difficulty with Ciaron. His theology has two aspects. One is resistance to power. I agree with this of course and willingly record my admiration for Ciaron's long struggle against Babylon. However equally important for Ciaron is the emphasis on repentance. I refuse this. I do not agree that we all sinned in East Timor. Those who sinned were those who had power to prevent what happened. The sinners were those who mobilised the butchers.

To talk of universal guilt and the need for universal repentance here is to draw attention away from those who have blood on their hands. Similarly I believe Billy Graham talked of universal sin at the massacre in My Lai to cover over the crimes of the US military in Vietnam. The people responsible for the rapes and massacres in My Lai were the leaders of the American Military-Industrial Complex. As always, it was the powerful who gave the go ahead for rampant evil.

Having said that, Ciaron's book was also difficult for me in that it was a powerful reminder to me that I too had forgotten to remember East Timor. Yet the invasion of East Timor in 1975 was the occasion for my first political protest in Australia. Called by the Communist Party of Australia, a few hundred of us gathered in King George Square on a hot summer day. I recall hearing Dan O'Neill speak for the first time. He talked with great feeling of the fires of resistance 'all along the archipelago'. Twenty-five years were to pass before his words came true.

We had come with our children that day and many of them stripped off and dived into the fountains.

The next day *The Courier Mail* coverage dealt not with the facts of the invasion or our protest against it. Instead, it concentrated on what kind of parents we were to let our children dance naked in the fountains. The implication was, of course, that we were not respectable people.

I was reminded of this coverage by a recent letter in the *Catholic Leader* attacking Ciaron. It was written by someone, who styled himself as 'respectable'. Again the implication was that, like us in 1975, Ciaron was not respectable. I think we all have to plead guilty in this instance. I know it is not in Ciaron's nature to enter a plea of guilty without at least a three-week trial. Nevertheless the simple truth is that in a world where it is respectable to plan and execute the murder of over a quarter of a million people, Ciaron O'Reilly is far from being a respectable person and for that he has my undying admiration.

Moreover the respectable letter writer would do well to ponder that when Christ charged through the temple, whip in hand, driving the money lenders before him, there is little doubt that he was not respectable. Indeed such was the depth of his non-respectability that he was ultimately tried in a court of law, found guilty and executed as a criminal by the respectable people of his day.

But of course the letter writer to the *Catholic Leader* has forgotten the past of the founder of his church. That church too has forgotten the message of the gospels and instead has opted for a shabby compromise with the existing state of affairs and the powerful few who benefit from it.

This brings me in turn to my final difficulty with Ciaron's book. He comes out of a tradition, theological and political, that I, as a Marxist, do not share. His mentor and example is the saintly Dorothy Day, the founder of the Catholic Worker movement. This anarcho-Christian movement has been extremely powerful in the United States. It is less so in Australia due to the especially degenerate nature of Australian Catholicism. The absolute alienation from the sacred, which is the true mark of today's Christian, is especially strong in Australia.

Thus, not one of Australia's Catholic leaders strikes me as being even remotely touched by holiness. The paradigmatic case here is surely the powerful Bishop Pell from Melbourne, a man who seems destined for a 'distinguished' career in the Vatican. Something of the measure of his humanity may be gained from the incident when he personally intervened to prevent nuns running safe injection programs for addicts in Sydney. The nuns aimed to save lives, but the good bishop remained resolutely respectable.

The truth though is that, here, I am comfortable in the contemplation of the likes of George Pell. Everything I say and hint at about him and his kind is true and transparently so. There is not one to gainsay me. Every word and deed of Pell and his colleagues confirm me in my opposition to his church and all of its works and pomp. But Ciaron's narrative eats into my comfort zone. It reminds me that perhaps I have assumed the moral high ground with a touch too much alacrity and maybe not without a good deal of smugness.

Ciaron's book provides nothing of the easy targets like Pell. As I have said, his mentor and example is the saintly Dorothy Day. She was a woman whose every moment was lived in quiet, non-violent opposition to the powerful and the respectable. Her influence is everywhere in this book and indeed in Ciaron's life. That, in truth, is the source of the considerable gulf between Ciaron and me. It seems to me that Ciaron dreams of repentance, reconciliation and forgiveness. By contrast I dream of *Dies Irae*. His thoughts are full of images of the sharing of bread and wine. Mine are of tumbrels and the dispensing of slow justice to the powerful.

But I will live with my difficulties with Ciaron's book. I will struggle with them for his stories have moved me deeply. His is nothing less than the simple chronicling of many little acts of kindness and of love by people who will never make it into the ranks of the respectable.

The highlight for me was the story of the four Ploughshare activists on trial in Liverpool for their attacks on a Hawk aircraft. Their names are Andrea Needham, Jo Wilson, Angie Zelter and Lotta Kronlid.

All honour to them. In the cockpit of the plane that they had disarmed, the women left a videotape explaining why they felt compelled to confront the evil of the arms trade.

In their stupidity, the prosecution played the tape to the jury. These ordinary, decent, working-class men and women were asked to listen to the tape that also included a plea from an East Timorese woman that said, 'Please stop your arms trade with Indonesia if you are really human'.

The jury was confidently expected by the powerful and the morally challenged to use this tape as evidence of guilt. Instead they were moved deeply and the tape became proof of the guilt of the rich and the powerful and all those who have profited from the trade in death. The subsequent acquittal of the four Ploughshare activists was greeted with great joy by their supporters and with fear and dismay by the powerful.

I cannot read Ciaron's book without shedding tears. Ciaron's act of remembering renews my faith in the basic decency of humanity. It strengthens my conviction that if ordinary people can only have access to the truth they will choose the side of goodness. For that I am profoundly grateful, and all the difficulties that this book (and Ciaron) have caused me are as nothing.

There is much more in the book that I can commend to the reader, but my prologue is in danger of overstaying its welcome. It is time that the main act was allowed on the stage. I will conclude with Walter Benjamin's great image of the *Angel of History*. It comes from his *Theses on the Philosophy of History*. In the second of these theses Benjamin argues that every generation is endowed with what he terms a '*weak* Messianic power'. Our coming was expected by the dead. There is a 'secret agreement' between them and us. They have a hope that we will redeem their suffering by remembering. It is within our power to perform that remembering. The past has a claim on this Messianic power but as Benjamin warns, and Ciaron's book amply testifies, the claim of the dead on our capacity to remember them cannot be settled cheaply.

In the Ninth Thesis we read of how the angel wishes to turn back and heal the wounds left by the slaughter bench of history.

But progress or capitalist modernity will not let it stay to remember and heal. It seems to me that Ciaron's book is best understood as an impulse to resist the forces of so-called progress and, instead, to witness to our humanity by remembering and to fulfil our commitment to the dead

> *Mein Flügel ist zum Schwung bereit*
> *Ich kehrte gern zuruck,*
> *Denn blieb ich auch lebendige Zeit,*
> *Ich hatte wenig Glück.*
> Gerhard Scholem
> *Gruss vom Angelus*

A Klee painting named '*Angelus Novus*' shows an angel looking as though he is about to move away from something he is fixedly contemplating. His eyes are staring, his mouth is open, his wings are spread. This is how one pictures the angel of history. His face is turned towards the past. Where we perceive a chain of events, he sees one single catastrophe which keeps piling wreckage upon wreckage, and hurls it in front of his feet. The angel would like to stay, awaken the dead, and make whole what has been smashed. But a storm is blowing from Paradise; it has got caught in his wings with such violence that the angel can no longer close them.

This storm irresistibly propels him into the future to which his back is turned, while the pile of debris before him grows skyward.

This storm is what we call progress. (Walter Benjamin)

Brisbane
7th August 2000

7

# 1  Australia

## 1.1  Arriving in East Timor

In late March 2000 I was released from Darwin jail, where along with Treena Lenthall I had completed a sixty-seven day sentence for disabling uranium mining equipment at the Jabiluka lease site. A few days after release we found ourselves on a troop laden Hercules heading for East Timor.

Setting foot in an East Timor free of the genocidal Indonesian military was the culmination of a seven year journey of resistance that had taken me from pouring blood in the boardroom of an Australian mining company to the Judges' chambers of the High Court in London. It was a journey of non-violent resistance and a journey of faith-based community with Brisbane suburbanites, Scousers of Liverpool and exiles from Los Palos, East Timor.

As we made our way out of the Díli airport, we were surprised to run into Kupa Lopez. Kupa had been one of the first of the young East Timorese exiles to land in Britain at the end of 1996. He came from Los Palos, as we use to say the 'South Armagh of East Timor', meaning strong in resistance and heavily militarised. Early in 1996, he had led student demonstrations in Jakarta and had sought refuge in the Australian Embassy, which he and a number of fellow East Timorese activists occupied for thirty days requesting political asylum in my country.

Their request was denied by the Australian Government, so

it was a wonderful opportunity that we could exchange the gifts and pathos of community and hospitality in England. As usual the movement was way ahead of the diplomats and bureaucrats.

Within a couple of years, there were about twenty exiled activists in Britain. These men, in their early and mid-20's, had been born on the eve and after the December 1975 invasion. Their lives and stories enfleshed the painful story of their people, their imprisonment and their torture. Some had witnessed the murder of their parents. Many had lost siblings to the Indonesian military. Some had gone to the mountains to join the guerrillas. Some had stayed in Díli involved in clandestine activities. Others had organised open demonstrations and occupations in Díli and Jakarta.

Living, working, resisting and sharing jail cells with these young men was an experience of evangelisation, an experience of awakening. Confronting the institutions, governments and corporations that oppress them and service me, the First World white male, was a healing and liberating experience.

As we left the airport, it became clear that this wasn't the East Timor we had all struggled for in the mountains, in the streets and in the jail cells. The main street of Díli seemed a constant parade of United Nations (UN) and Western charity bureaucrats, a circular procession of expensive four wheel drives.

The display of economic apartheid was stunning: a Western UN/charity representative would cruise by travelling solo in a huge four wheel drive followed by overcrowded minibuses with East Timorese clinging by their toes and fingertips to the outside. We had to remind ourselves, better this circus than the Soeharto slaughterhouse!

Evidence of what had preceded this scene by only six months was abundant. The entire central business district and beyond was charred, trashed and gutted. From all reports this was duplicated throughout the towns and villages of the countryside.

The political scene was similarly trashed. This was not Nicaragua following the fall of the United States-backed Somoza regime in the early 1980's.

East Timor had been 'liberated' and occupied by the same

forces that facilitated the twenty-four year Indonesian military's occupation and attempted genocide. The jury is still out (in fact hasn't and probably won't be formed) on Australian, US and World Bank complicity in the scorched earth events of September 1999.

US Admiral Blair was in town while we were there, the same man who refrained from getting his friend Wiranto to call off the militias in 1999, but rather sent upbeat cables looking forward to joint Hawaiian holidays and restored US training of Indonesian military.

The CNRT are not Sandanistas who are an unwieldy ambiguous grouping, initiated at the request of the West, without a clear program. No. The CNRT offers little counterweight to UN colonisation. The UN is now running colonies in Bosnia, Kosovo and East Timor. Last year a US official declared that 'East Timor is Australia's Haiti'. Have a close look at Haiti today after six years of US 'liberation' and start to worry for East Timor!

The economic apartheid is in sharp relief. East Timorese score jobs as drivers, cleaners and translators at five dollars a day, while their Western counterparts are on 'big bucks'. Western aid agencies are not the *Sandalistas* of the 1980's. They are, by and large not here on advice from the locals, but to impose a Western agenda.

There is very little social integration between the Western employees and the East Timorese. We found the soldiers on foot patrol a lot friendlier than the aid and charity workers who seemed cocooned in their Toyotas. We went to the Stadium Díli on the weekend to watch the football. We were some of the few malai faces in the crowd. Of the eight teams, mostly sponsored by Western aid agencies, only two malai players took to the field. Not a good sign for the World Game!

The floating Hotel Olympia moored downtown stood as a symbol that most of the international money marked for East Timor is heading offshore and into the pockets of Western bureaucracies and careerists.

There was a US coffee consortium developing a monopoly. There were large numbers of rural youth gravitating to Díli looking for work and hanging around in a milieu of 80% unemployment and growing frustration.

The militias remain, bankrolled and active on the border playing out their role in the internal power machinations of Indonesia.

## *1.2  Why Write this Reflection?*

The people on the street are wonderful. The spirit is strong and joyous, amazing considering all they have been through over the long haul and in the recent short term. The material poverty is extreme, yet there is a wealth of culture and spirit. There is an abundance of dignity and an absence of drugs, begging and prostitution.

We met with student activists who have no campus or classes, who are critical of the present political scene but remain hopeful and active and know they have a long struggle before them for independence. The struggle before them is against the same forces that supported the twenty-four year Indonesian occupation this time with 'nice cop' pretensions.

Milan Kundera, the Czech dissident, once reflected, 'the struggle between power and people is the struggle between remembering and forgetting!' A friend remarks that memory maybe a bigger issue in a frontier culture like White Australia where the present and future looms large. In his refusal to apologise to the Aborigines, Prime Minister Howard denies any link between the past and present. It is important for him also to suppress the memory of the support from the Australian Government, military and corporations for the brutal and genocidal Indonesian military's occupation of East Timor.

This brutality could no longer be denied in the mass

coverage of post-ballot events and massacres of September 1999. In order to fashion a Western present and future for East Timor it is important to generate a popular amnesia, as the Australian military are celebrated rather than confronted with their twenty-four year aiding and abetting complicity in the genocidal war on East Timor, an Australian complicity that continues to be duplicated in West Papua and elsewhere.

This account is to remember some of that past, some of the non-violent resistance and the beliefs underlying it when East Timor was under fire. These are some of the stories of small groups of people in Australia and England who struggled to hear the cries of the East Timorese, see what was causing their pain and speak truth to power with a clarity of sight, hearing and speech, the very healings we are promised in the gospels. This reflection is not complete.

There are many other stories to be told that we can draw on what will contribute to a dissident memory. As Native American Leslie Marmon Silko reminds us,

> 'I will tell you something about stories', he said.
> 'They aren't just entertainment
> Don't be fooled,
> They are all we have, you see,
> all we have to fight off illness and death.
> You don't have anything
> if you don't have stories
> Their evil is mighty
> but it can't stand up to our stories,
> So they try to destroy the stories
> let the stories be confused or forgotten,
> They would like that
> They would be happy
> Because we would be defenceless then...'
>
> Leslie Marmon Silko
> *Ceremony*

In 1993 I was deported from the US after serving thirteen

14

months imprisonment for non-violent resistance to the 1991 Gulf Massacre. Along with Moana Cole, Sue Frankel and Bill Streit, I had participated in the disarmament of a combat ready B-52 Bomber in upstate New York, fifteen days before George Bush's deadline.

We managed to put the B-52 out of action for the length of the massacre, were charged with conspiracy and destruction of government property, tried and imprisoned. During my time in a twenty-four man cage in a Texas prison, I remember remembering East Timor. A friend had sent me some pages from the New York Times and there was a photo of East Timorese on the march in Portugal in response to a November 1991 massacre of some 250 people in the Santa Cruz cemetery in Díli.

I remember lying on my bunk and thinking 'Oh the East Timorese, are they still around?'

I remember wearing a badge to high school in the mid-70's. It showed a Fretilin flag. Another demanded, 'East Timor: Indonesian Troops Out Now!'

I remember a poster near our school protesting the denial of a visa to an East Timorese activist wishing to do a speaking tour.

I remember the Catholic-dominated Special Branch Police snooping around our Young Christian Students' house.

I remember them pulling church strings to have the East Timor office evicted.

I remember forgetting the cries of the East Timorese.

The censorship in Australia concerning the war on East Timor was so complete that even activists in the relatively large Australian peace movement of the 1980's rarely thought of East Timor or mentioned it. We knew a lot more about the wars on faraway El Salvador and Nicaragua than we did about this small nation 300 miles north of our coastline. There was a conscious campaign to forget East Timor and it was largely successful. As Fr. Frank Cordaro would say it was a 'cultivated ignorance'. A lot of effort had to go into ignoring genocide in a neighbouring country.

For the most part, the Australian peace movement slept through the genocide in East Timor. The Australian media, that had five of its journalists slain by the Indonesian military at the outset of the invasion, was cooperative in the cover-up. The Australian Catholic Church maintained its silence in the face of the genocide in this neighbouring Catholic nation.

So, appreciating that we have forgotten once before, I feel obliged to put down the memories of our recent resistance before they, too, are denied by a triumphalist, self-interested Australian Government which is yet to confront its twenty-four year complicity in the mass murder of a people.

What struck me most clearly on arriving back in Australia in mid 1993 was that the same governments that had executed the massacre of the Iraqi people in 1991 on the 'moral' basis of stopping a larger nation (Iraq) annexing a smaller one (Kuwait) had been financing and facilitating the invasion of East Timor by the Indonesian dictatorship for over 20 years.

The filming of the November 1991 Santa Cruz cemetery massacre by Max Stahl, the smuggling of the footage out of East Timor by Saskia Kouwenberg and the documentary 'Death of a Nation', by John Pilger had pretty much single handedly put East Timor back on the map. As the East Timorese would tell you, such massacres from the air or by ground forces wielding Western weapons were common enough. The only difference with Santa Cruz was that it was captured on film and exposed to the world.

## *1.3* *Community and Resistance*

In 1993 in Brisbane we began to vigil (to stay awake while society slumbers) at places of death linked to the continued war on the East Timorese people.

Some of us had hooked up originally in the late 1970's during the extreme police repression in Queensland under the Bjelke-Petersen Government. After surviving the rise and fall of civil liberties and anti-nuclear movements, we took a long hard look at who we were. Philosophically we were Christian-anarchist-pacifist. We attempted to combine the praxis of intentional community, hospitality to the poor and non-violent resistance to the institutions of death and privilege. We linked with the Catholic Worker movement on the move since 1933 in the US and the faith-based Ploughshares movement. We took a cue from Jesus to resist the temptations of wealth, power and status with which he had wrestled and which he had rejected in the desert. We were careful not to be seduced into managing the poor or managing dissent, but chose to operate on the margins where the spirit and conscience have room to move.

Throughout the 1980's we had managed to muster non-violent resistance to nuclear warship visits, nuclear war-fighting bases, Boggo Road maximum security prison, restrictions on free speech, Roxby Downs uranium mine, gentrification and evictions in our neighbourhood that accompanied the World Fair, and solidarity with aboriginal demands for land rights and justice.

Since 1989, Catholic Workers began to celebrate various liturgical feast days with non-violent resistance at the Canungra Land Warfare Centre and School of Military Intelligence where Indonesian, Thai, Filipino and Papua New Guinea troops are regularly trained in techniques of waging war on their poor. In Brisbane's inner city West End, for over a decade, we had experimented with community living and Catholic Worker houses of hospitality and founded Justice Products, a retail outlet for co-operatively made goods.

By the end of 1994 we decided to start a resistance community primarily focused on solidarity with East Timor. We located ourselves in a section of St. Mary's church house, South Brisbane. St. Mary's is a centre of liberal Catholicism in Brisbane located next to the conservatively run St. Vincent de Paul homeless shelter. It was interesting to have Australian Catholic conservatives, liberals and radicals all on the same block, frequented by the homeless and near to the city's towers of power.

We named the house after Greg Shackleton, an Australian journalist who was one of the first victims of the Indonesian invasion of East Timor in 1975. In October 1975, he had been slain along with four other Australian-based journalists in the border town of Balibo by a raiding party of Indonesian troops. We felt Greg, a privileged white Australian, was someone very much like us who had suffered very much like the East Timorese. He had shared risk with those in the firing line to speak truth to power. We saw him as a relevant role model and wished to honour his memory in defiance of the Australian Government's campaign to forget it. Greg's widow, Shirley, came from Melbourne to officially open the house. This was preceded by a public meeting of 500 people. We were committed to publicly and non-violently confronting Australia's military, economic and diplomatic contribution to the war on East Timor and attempted to invite others to do the same.

Our community spiritual life was nourished by a weekly liturgy and open house, and by a weekly study of Ched Meyer's 'Who Will Roll Away the Stone?' a companion to his earlier biblical commentary on Mark's gospel 'Binding the Strongman'.

After six months, the group moved on to a study of John's gospel using Wes Howard Brook's commentary 'Becoming Children of God' and later a study of the Book of Revelation using Anthony Gwyther's commentary 'Unveiling Empire'.[1]

The basic approach of these theologians is that out of oppressed Third World communities such as East Timor there will come a 'Theology of Liberation' but out of First World communities such as ours, privileged by imperialism and a global system of exploitation, there must come a 'Theology of Repentance and Resistance'.

## *1.4  High Theft and Exorcism on the 23rd Floor*

One of the seminal images of Australia's betrayal of the East Timorese people is the champagne-popping signing of the Timor Gap Treaty by Foreign Ministers Gareth Evans and Ali Alatas while flying over the Timor Sea in 1989. This act of piracy over the high seas flew in the face of Australian apologetics that East Timor was economically an 'unviable state'. Given that the UN had passed ten resolutions calling for immediate Indonesian withdrawal and that Australia was the only nation to recognise the Indonesian annexation, this was a most illegal act. As we saw it, it was an act of high theft, of armed robbery, carried out by a genocidal military equipped by the West.

Many Australian-based mining companies moved to exploit the arrangement including Royal Dutch Shell, Chevron, BHP, Santos, Nippon Oil, Phillips, Saagas, Petroz, Enterprise and the Western Mining Company. Indeed, sunny Brisbane hosted many companies carrying out the systematic theft of Third World resources: CRA that had been forced off the island of Bougainville, BHP that continues to pollute the Ok Tedi River in Papua New Guinea, and the Freeport Mine imposed on West Papua and supplied from North Queensland. We decided to make Petroz our focus. Petroz was headquartered in Brisbane and was pursuing an aggressive Timor Sea drilling program.

We tried to engage Petroz with dialogue, vigilance and

liturgy outside its high-rise doors but we seemed to be bouncing off unable to seriously engage. The rubber wasn't hitting the road. Their 23rd floor office in this tower of concrete and steel from which they operated appeared so sterile and distant from the blood being spilt. Their public relations strategy viewed dialogue as a means of managing dissent. We decided to reach into the symbols and sacraments of our tradition to speak some truth to power. From our studies of Scripture we had increasingly come to view Jesus' practise of exorcism as a dynamic confrontation with the powers of death and domination in the world, such themes as are explored in depth by the theologian Walter Wink.

On the anniversary of the Díli Massacre we gathered in Brisbane's Anzac Square. Many of us there had been carrying out such actions over the past seventeen years. Four of us gained access to the basement car park of the Colonial Mutual Building while others set up a vigil in Queen Street at the front of the building. We rode the elevator to the 23rd floor which opened on to the Petroz offices. As the lift doors opened, my brother Sean engaged the Petroz secretary in conversation about East Timor while the rest of us strode past into the boardroom. We had brought with us containers of human blood that we had donated to the action. We poured this blood over the boardroom table and the Petroz logo to symbolise the East Timorese blood that had been spilt as a result of the corporate decisions made around this table. We pasted the office walls and exploration maps with photographs of Timorese slain, starving and wounded. We then carried out a rite of deliverance, or exorcism, naming the spirits of Petroz for what they were, spillers of blood, reapers of profit, destroyers of villages, homes and lives. We cast out any control Petroz and its agents of state and law had over our behaviour, any hopes they maintained for our silence and complicity in the face of 200,000 Timorese dead. We then knelt in prayer.

We prayed as an act of radical disillusionment with a culture that demanded the genocide of the East Timorese and our accompanying silence. As Meyers points out,

'It is in Mark's gospel instructive that Jesus invites

21

the disciples to pray on just two occasions. One is after his dramatic repudiation of the Temple as a 'house of thieves' (11:17) There Jesus urges his disciples to envision a different world in which the exploitative temple state is overthrown and replaced by the community practice of reconciliation (11:24) The other instance occurs just before Jesus is about to be seized by the same State's security forces, where he summons his followers to prayer as a way of 'staying awake' (14:32-42) Markan prayer is clearly more than a private exercise in piety or meditation. It seems to be a way of engaging the Powers in the apocalyptic struggle over history; that it is why it is the site of contested loyalty from the wilderness to Gethsemane.'[2]

As the police arrived in the boardroom, I welcomed them with the greeting, 'Officers, officers, we're so glad you're here! There's been an armed robbery. Petroz is stealing oil from the Timor Strait at gunpoint. Over 200,000 Timorese and five Australians have been murdered. We've got to do something!'

Unfortunately the police stepped over nineteen years of genocide and 200,000 dead and ordered us to vacate the building. Lisa Bridle, seven months pregnant stood up and was escorted out. Jim Dowling and I refused to move. We were handcuffed tightly behind our backs, pressure holds were applied to our necks and wrist-locks were applied to get us to walk. We continued to refuse and let our bodies fall limp. It was a painful exit. We were finally loaded into a police van, taken to the watch house, charged with wilful damage and hindering police.

In the opening months of 1995, we decided to commit ourselves to a Lenten discipline of fasting and prayer in solidarity with the suffering of East Timor.

We opened the season of repentance with a vigil and street theatre in the City Mall on Ash Wednesday. The performers then lead a procession to Military Offices in Edward St. We were accompanied on our journey by members of the Queensland Police Riot squad.

On our arrival at the Edward Street offices, speeches were

made regarding Australia's involvement (through military training and arms supplies) in low intensity conflict wars in Bougainville, West Papua and East Timor. The procession then moved on to the Queen St. headquarters of Petroz. The company at that time was awaiting the ruling of the World Court on the legality of their activities under International Law.

Over one hundred folks gathered on the steps of the Colonial Mutual Building that housed Petroz offices to celebrate an Ash Wednesday mass. The burning of the Petroz annual report provided the ash for the ceremony. Following the liturgy a group of people began a vigil throughout the night outside Petroz. This vigil was maintained on a one-hour-a-day basis throughout Lent.

## 1.5   The Counter-Terrorist Squad Comes a Calling!

The phone call came a few days after our Ash Wednesday liturgy on the steps of the Petroz Mining Company. The caller indicated that he had attended the liturgy and wanted to discuss with me more about our activities regarding East Timor. I agreed to meet him that afternoon at the Sitting Duck Cafe. Before concluding our phone conversation, he informed me that he worked for the Queensland Police Service and would be bringing someone from the Air Force with him.

Allan, Dale and I ordered our coffees and our meeting began. It became immediately obvious that both men were present on a professional basis. There was no crisis of conscience here! It also became apparent that our friend from the Queensland Police Service was well read, on me, and on my past peace activism in the US and Australia.

I began to feel increasingly like a sitting duck myself, so I guess I was in the right place! I shared with them my fears that they were setting me up. In the absence of any terrorists, 'anti-terrorist' experts often created terrorists to justify their careers, budgets, promotions and existence.

I cited the examples of Ananda Marga, the Guilford Four, Birmingham Six and Father Brian Gore. They responded that this was not what this meeting was about.

Being of humble disposition, I tried the 'enough about me,

more about you!' turn of conversation. I asked if he was aware of a file being retained by the Anti-Terrorist Squad on me. He said he could neither confirm nor deny whether such a file was being retained. I asked if he worked for the section of the police service that retained such files. He confirmed that he did, this being the 'Counter-Terrorist Section of the Queensland Police Service'.

I asked him if he was aware that the Catholic Worker is a pacifist movement. He was. I asked how such a file on me or surveillance of the Ash Wednesday liturgy could be justified on the basis of counter-terrorism. I asked if he was aware of reports that the Australian Defence Department had been passing information on the Catholic Worker community to the Indonesian Government, making our members vulnerable to Indonesian operatives in Australia. He said he was aware of these reports. I wanted to know what his Counter-Terrorist Section of the Queensland Police Service was doing about investigating such reports. What were they are doing about protecting Australian citizens from a security force that has slain five Australian journalists, 200,000 East Timorese Catholics and over half a million of their own people? Given what a more mainstream French Government did to a more mainstream Greenpeace organisation, this should have been of some concern.

At this point in the discussion the Air Force dimension kicked in. The Queensland Police officer read a long list of military bases where the Catholic Worker community had carried out non-violent actions: Cabarlah, Canungra, Nurrungar, Pine Gap, Harewood (NZ), Griffiss (USA), Richmond and Watsonia. Compacted and rattled off like that, it sounded quite impressive.

He asked, 'We've always wondered why you have never been to Amberley?'

They were wondering what we had planned for the imminent arrival of American F-16 fighters, KC-135 refuelers for the 'Downunder 1995' joint military exercises, all planes that had been used extensively in the 1991 Gulf Massacre. I was a little embarrassed that we didn't have anything planned and that we were only marginally aware of their arrival.

I replied that we weren't Gandhians, so I didn't feel obliged to tell them what we were going to do. I assured both of them that we were pacifists and conducted our public actions with a strict non-violent discipline.

The Air Force security stated that his job 'is to make Amberley a safe place!'

I replied, 'Well my suggestion is for you to begin by removing all the explosives from the area and deny entry to any hi-tech weapons of mass destruction.'

This was answered by a sigh of exhaustion.

For about 50 minutes I attempted to discuss with these two experts on 'terror' and 'security' the subjects of their expertise. Are the sources of terror more likely to be found at our Ash Wednesday liturgy or the Canungra Jungle Warfare Training Centre where Indonesian troops are occasionally put through their paces?

In that month a US nuclear submarine carrying Polaris warheads pulled into Brisbane to pick up the elite Special Air Services of the Australian Army for exercises.

A week later, Indonesian paratroopers, the same folks that jumped, landed and massacred in West Papua and East Timor, were in the skies over Rockhampton. Were these organisations that have such a history of terror and stench of death, under surveillance?

Were the F-16's, KC-135's and Phantoms that were used extensively in the Gulf Massacre of January/February 1991, when over 88,500 tons of explosives were dropped on the people of Iraq, making us any more secure by their presence? Was it not the case that these hi-tech weapons had little to do with 'security' or 'defence' but were in fact the muscle that enforces global theft by transnational corporations sanctioned by the United States?

Had the Middle East become any more secure since the orgy of death carried out by these weapon systems? I told them that when we had non-violently disarmed a war-ready B-52 Bomber in New York State, that we had exposed the double illusion 'the weapons are secure/they secure us'.

So as we parted company I couldn't help but feel that the warlords, corporations and governments that rule had made sitting ducks of us all in our own way. To the empire, Allan, Dale and I were equally expendable.

I quite liked Allan and Dale. We shared moments of humour and humanity over the fifty minutes. I have a religious belief that our lives are sacred, as sacred as the Timorese, as Saddam's, Bill's, those on death rows and in firing lines. I believe the bureaucracies they serve are the wielders of terror and fonts of insecurity in our world.

On the morning of March 21 1995, 40,000 Turkish troops, funded, trained and informed by the US, invaded Northern Iraq to wipe out Kurdish villagers. Turkish pilots were flying US supplied F- 16's into combat. US aircraft and satellites were providing constant intelligence and targeting information.

Also that morning, fifteen friends of the Catholic Workers accompanied Anne Rampa and myself to Amberley Air Force Base. We attempted to make our way to the American F-16's and KC-135 Refuelers in transit to US bases in Southern Turkey. These planes stated mission was to enforce the crippling sanctions policy that was (and continues) costing thousands of Iraqi lives through starvation and disease. Anne and I carried a basketful of food, medical supplies, a hammer and a 'home handyman's guide to disarmament'.

About five feet into the base we were blocked by Australian Air Force personnel. We then blocked the entrance to the base. The gates were chained shut behind us. After some time a vehicle of US pilots attempted to gain access through the exit gate. I moved over to sit in front of their car and was arrested. Anne and her four month old son, Joseph, were taken into custody shortly after.

These are the gifts we believe can bring real security to our world and counter terror; community, responsibility and non-violent resistance. The illusion fed by the State's security forces finds its full expressions of terror in the faces of the children of Kurdistan and East Timor.

As Albert Camus reflected in 1948 on the Church's silence and abstraction in the face of preparations for WWII:

'For a long time during those frightful years I waited for a great voice to speak up (in the Church). I, an unbeliever? Precisely. For I knew that the spirit would be lost if it did not offer a cry of condemnation when faced with force...What the world expects of Christians is that Christians should speak out loud and clear...That they should get away from abstraction and confront the bloodstained face history has taken on today. The grouping we need is a grouping of people resolved to speak out clearly and pay up personally.'

## 1.6  *Marketable Massacre - Low Intensity Conflict*

B y the end of the Vietnam War, those in power had learnt their lessons and were deciding how their wars would be prosecuted in the future. The 'Vietnam Syndrome' would be one of the few restraining factors on US power. The syndrome could be defined as the domestic conflict brought about by revulsion at US casualties.

By 1972, the US Government had conceded to domestic opposition, stopped the draft and began US troop withdrawal. The domestic peace movement collapsed in response to this victory. However, the US military complemented this development with an escalation of the air war and a Vietnamisation of the ground war.

In the post-Vietnam War period the US has waged its imperial wars with hi-tech overkill from Grenada to Panama to Iraq to the Balkans with maximum damage to civilian infrastructure and minimum US casualties. This military technique is called 'escalation dominance'. It guarantees that the US can escalate to the next level of violence if ever challenged, all the way to thermo nuclear war.

The day-to-day maintenance of an empire of client states that guarantees the global theft of resources and exploitation of slave labour is through the military strategy known as 'low intensity conflict'.

In real terms this means that instead of risking American, European and Australian lives, Third World boys get to do the killing and dying for us. We equip, train and arm them and the killing and dying grinds on with little recognition or resistance in First World nations which benefit from this global armed robbery.

For whatever reason, tactical (secure passage for US shipping through the Timor Sea) or economic (the oil offshore of East Timor), President Ford and Secretary State Kissinger gave their blessing while in Jakarta two days before the December 1975 invasion of East Timor. The Soeharto dictatorship was a child of the US performing the same role as Pinochet in Chile, Mobutu in Zaire, the Shah in Iran; the list is endless!

Australia's military complicity with the Indonesian invasion of East Timor was evident from the outset. The Defence Signals Directorate base near Darwin would have intercepted all Indonesian military communications in the lead up to the December 7 1975 invasion, including the October 19 massacre of the five Australian based journalists. This passive silence was complemented by the proactive suppression of radio communications between Fretilin and Australian sympathisers in the Northern Territory.

The East Timorese put up significant armed resistance to the invasion. A resistance that was broken in the late 1970's by the use of Western warplanes, including Broncos supplied by the US and Hawks supplied by Britain. By the early 1980's, Fretilin had been reduced to small guerrilla bands and the Indonesian military settled in for a low intensity conflict.

Australia's contribution to this low intensity conflict was significant. The élite Australian Special Air Services offered annual training to the psychopaths of the élite Indonesian Kopassus units at their base in Perth. Soeharto's son-in-law, General Prabowo, headed Kopassus. Kopassus was extensively deployed in East Timor, West Papua and Aceh and was responsible for many atrocities.

South of Brisbane, in the Gold Coast hinterland, Canungra Land Warfare Training Centre offered counter-insurgency training to Indonesian, Papua New Guinea, Thai and Filipino troops.

Along with the military's downtown Edward St. offices it provided a focus for our resistance to Australia's military complicity in the slaughter in East Timor. 1995 was also the 50th anniversary of WWII and the Federal Government ran an 'Australia Remembers' campaign to celebrate the historic occasion. Given the history of East Timorese support for Australia troops we found this particularly ironic.

Indeed the Sparrow Unit that was offered sanctuary by the East Timorese from Japanese forces was later to evolve in to the Australian SAS now training the Kopassus killers of the East Timorese. As Sparrow Unit pulled out of East Timor they dropped a leaflet in Portuguese promising the East Timorese 'we will never forget you!' The East Timorese lost 40,000 lives in supporting Australian troops.

1995 saw over 500 Indonesian troops welcomed to the Northern Territory and Queensland to participate in the $64 million Kangaroo 1995 exercises along with 15,750 personnel from the Australian military and 2,540 troops from Papua New Guinea, Malaysia, Singapore, Britain and the US. It was the largest military exercise to be held in Australia. The area of the exercise stretched from Broome through Tennant Creek to Cairns and to the north of that line including the Australian fishing zone.

We concluded our Lenten campaign with a Timor Stations of the Cross where we carried a cross and gave reflections at Santoz Mining Co., Petroz Mining Co., the Department of Foreign Affairs, Garuda Airlines and the Military offices in Edward St. On Holy Thursday we gathered at the Defence Office to protest against the Australian Government's continued training of Indonesian soldiers.

Dressed in black and wearing names of East Timorese slain in the Díli Massacre, Sr. Kay McFadden, Jim Dowling and I occupied the Defence Office. Others gathered outside with a long list of those killed at the 1991 Díli Massacre, many mere teenagers. These lists were to form the cross venerated at St. Mary's during Good Friday mass. After an eight-hour occupation, Kay, Jim and I were arrested and charged with trespass.

We were processed from the watch house in the evening and arrived back at St Mary's during the Holy Thursday liturgy which provided a powerful interplay between the liturgy of the Church and streets.

A week before the Kangaroo 1995 exercises we opened the 'East Timor 1942 - 1992' photographic exhibition in the church. The 104 photographs covered a 50-year period capturing images of people in towns and rural communities, the flora, the Portuguese and the Indonesians, spanning pristine beauty to the horrors of war. During this time, Bob Cunningham conducted a week long fast at the Canungra Land Warfare Centre in repentance for Australia's training and arming of troops who have killed East Timorese.

Over the course of the week, Bob was joined by a number of supporters and had many interactions with members of the Australian military based at Canungra. On the eve of the K-95 exercises we organised a 'Speak Out for East Timor' with Shirley Shackleton who reflected on the murder of her husband and the massacre of the East Timorese. 500 people gathered to hear Shirley share her story in Brisbane for the first time.

The following day Shirley and a dozen members of the East Timorese community were joined by sixty folks in marching on Canungra. We were led by a huge kangaroo puppet with a 'Stop Kangaroo 1995' sign as we proceeded to the gates of Canungra. At the entrance, a coffin of 'Australian Government betrayal and broken promises' was filled with mementoes. Shirley spoke of her husband's death at the hands of Indonesian troops and Barb Crossing told of how the lives of her father, uncle and guardian were saved by the courage of the East Timorese people during WWII.

The presence of the East Timorese community spoke powerfully to exile, genocide and defiant survival. Those present planted crosses with the names of Timorese dead at the gate. Sr. Kay McFadden, Damien LeGoullon and Lisa Bridle carried the coffin on to the base heading for the School of Military Intelligence. They were arrested and charged with trespass and refusal to leave Commonwealth property.

In the following years a variety of resistance actions were carried out at Canungra. These notably included a 100 km 'Journey of Peace' walk in mid 1997, from the Military office in Brisbane to the base, concluding with trespass and arrests.

Following the court appearance of this group, on the 1997 anniversary of the invasion of East Timor, were the arrests of nineteen people including a priest, senate candidate, a lecturer, an East Timorese exile, a former army major and Saskia who had smuggled the Díli massacre footage out of East Timor. In court, all resisters attempted to put the war on East Timor on trial, calling expert witnesses, cross examining military personnel, providing personal testimony and submitting the 1942 leaflet airdropped by retreating Australian forces promising the East Timorese 'Your Friends Will Not Forget You!'

## *1.7* **Sanctuary of the Church**

n unusual series of events lead to the most productive
relationship between the Greg Shackleton Catholic
Worker and the St. Mary's Church. In mid 1995, the
Portuguese Government took Australia to the World Court over the
illegality of the Timor Gap Treaty. Indonesia does not recognise the
court, so Australia was the sole defendant. The lawyers for the
Australian Government argued that Portugal 'no longer has any
legal claim or responsibility in the region in respect to East Timor'.
The World Court merely concluded that it could not rule in this
matter due to lack of recognition by Indonesia.

Shortly after this case, the French Government began testing
nuclear weapons in the Pacific. This ignited a popular response in
the streets of Australia. In a rare phenomenon, tens of thousands of
Australians took to the streets mobilised by mainstream
organisations and media outlets.

The Labor Government did its best to surf this wave of
resentment to the French Government's resumption of nuclear
testing. The Labor hacks managed to define the issue in NIMBY
(not-in-my-backyard) and Franco-phobic terms. It took Jacques
Chirac to state the obvious, 'If the Australian Government are so
opposed to our nuclear weapons program, they should stop selling
us their uranium!'

This period of popular mobilisation of dissent came at an

unfortunate time for the sycophantic Keating/Evans Labor Government, as the Indonesian ambassador had resigned and was due to be replaced. Soeharto put forward the Díli Massacre cheerleader General Mantiri as his nomination. The rarely roused Australian public turned its attention to this outrage and barked back 'No Way!' to the government. For most of the second half of the year, Indonesia refused to appoint an ambassador. Payback was demanded. Gareth Evans decided to deliver in late October by promising the deportation of 1,300 East Timorese from Australia. He announced that the government would be recommending to the Australian Refugee Review Tribunal rejection of refugee status to the 1,800 East Timorese presently seeking refugee status in Australia.

The majority of the 1,300 had arrived in the previous few years by means of overstaying visiting visas or making the perilous boat trip to Darwin. The East Timorese were arguing that their lives and liberty were under threat from the Indonesian military occupying their country; with over 200,000 slain they had ample evidence. Evans didn't make a counter-argument to this claim. Instead he attempted to conjure a technicality, contrary to his government's argument put at the World Court in relation to East Timorese oil. He tried the 'all East Timorese are really Portuguese, so ship them to Europe' thrust.

The threatened mass deportations were another face of Australia's contribution to the war on East Timor. To remove a dissident expatriate community, many bearing the fresh scars of torture and the loss of loved ones, to a faraway continent was no small offering by Evans. Indonesian Foreign Minister Alatas expressed predictable excitement with the prospect.

We decided to approach the larger St. Mary's congregation with the proposal to declare sanctuary of the church for the East Timorese threatened with deportation. The rediscovery of this ancient tradition, and the simple notion that sanctuaries should be sanctuaries, was pregnant with possibility. The ancient notion that holy sites be regarded, by their very nature, as places of refuge is not uniquely Christian.

Sanctuary was more or less formalised practice in Egypt, Syria, Greece and Rome. Political fugitives, debtors and slaves on the run all passed beyond the pale of revenge by making it into the precincts of a recognised shrine.[3]

In the Christian tradition, sanctuary has its roots in the early pacifist church and its role as intermediary in disputes ('lest innocent blood be shed'), as fugitives were protected, slaves interceded for and debtors sheltered until a bargain could be made with those seeking vengeance or forgiveness given. Rediscovering the sanctuary as sanctuary has often been a 'confessional' and clarifying moment in the history of the church. Its declaration celebrates the sovereignty of God (of peace, justice, love, life) in history, marking the limit of civil authority. It was clearly a confessional moment for an Australian church in relation to its East Timorese neighbours who had experienced twenty years of genocide. It was also a confessional moment in relation to successive Australian governments that have actively and passively contributed to this genocide.

A government that now stood poised to slam the door in the face of those fleeing a situation we helped construct, diplomatically, economically and militarily. An East Timorese people who offered sanctuary to Australian troops fleeing Japanese forces in the 1940's. An East Timorese people who were daily facing the perils of offering sanctuary to those declared fugitive in their own homeland by a brutal military occupation force.

Although the function, practice and theology of sanctuary is not to be circumscribed by civil acknowledgment, in the history of the church, Christian sanctuary has enjoyed various seasons of legal recognition.

The period and place where sanctuary was most formalised was England, where for several centuries at any given time there were more than a thousand people under protection of the Church's peace. The ecclesiastical turf was carefully set forth, and elaborate procedures for the sanctuary seeker obtained.

There have been other occasions, however, when the sanctuary of the Church has been swamped by the State.

In January 1933, the altar of Magdeburg Cathedral and many other churches in Germany were smothered in swastika flags. As American bombs rained on the children of Vietnam, Panama and Iraq, the stars and stripes could be found on altars throughout the US.

For the most part, however, the practice of sanctuary has been fraught with risk. This has been the story from the underground railroad in the US which hid escaping slaves to the martyrs of the French village of Le Chambon who secreted Jews in the 1940's to the 1980's movement responding to Central American refugees fleeing north from US sponsored wars.

On October 28 1991, Sabastio Ranel, an East Timorese student, was seeking sanctuary in the Motael church grounds when he was slain by Indonesian troops. By the time his November 12 funeral procession reached the Santa Cruz cemetery it was transformed by the same troops, into the bloodbath of the Díli Massacre. Over 200 unarmed East Timorese were butchered that day. Some of the survivors were now on Gareth Evans deportation hit list.

On the first Sunday of November at St. Mary's, Fr. Peter Kennedy, who was a navy chaplain mobilised to Darwin at the time of the Indonesian invasion, presided over the sanctuary mass. Barbara Crossing spoke of how the East Timorese had offered sanctuary to her father, uncle and guardian at the cost of 40,000 East Timorese lives during WWII. Afonso Corte Real spoke of how his elders were slain for offering Australians sanctuary and how his people were now pleading to Australians for the gift of sanctuary. During the ceremony over 400 parishioners circled the church in a symbolic declaration of sanctuary for the 1,300 East Timorese threatened with deportation and all those fleeing an invasion Australia continued to sponsor. We were joined by four religious orders and fifteen parishes around Australia. A number of Trade Unions and Bishop Cremon declared sanctuary on the same day. Coverage of the sanctuary movement appeared in Australian, Malaysian, Indonesian and Vietnamese newspapers. Foreign Affairs Minister Gareth Evans was visibly shaken when interviewed about the declarations.

Due largely to the organising efforts of Josephite nuns in Sydney and solidarity activists in Melbourne, the major population centres of the East Timorese community in Australia, the sanctuary network grew to 10,000 strong by the late 1990's. Joined by a number of WWII veterans, Catholic Bishop Hilton-Deakin addressed a huge demonstration in Melbourne encouraging civil disobedience to the government's intentions of deportation. Weeks before the Keating/Evans Government was voted out we managed to gatecrash a pre-election Labor Party event and confront Gareth around the table in a good twenty-minute interchange concerning the immorality and consequences of his actions. He seemed sophisticated, arrogant, unrepentant and resigned to electoral defeat.

The sanctuary movement was certainly effective in slowing down the deportation process, along with the Federal Court rulings in 1997 and 1998 finding that the right to Portuguese nationality and Portuguese 'protection' was not effective and that the East Timorese had the right to seek refuge status here. The new Howard/Ruddock Government attempted new legal initiatives to make it less likely that the asylum seekers would gain refugee status. They refused any extension to the 2,000 East Timorese refugees who were offered a temporary 'safe haven' visa following the September 1999 massacres. On the same day the Australian Government welcomed home the first rotation of Australian troops from their East Timor assignment, they forcibly returned these refugees to minimal infrastructure, scarce shelter, little food, and rampant disease in the middle of monsoon season.

## *1.8 Busting out of the Locked Room!*

On January 29 1996, Greg Shackleton House received a phone call from the Ploughshares network in England to celebrate that Lotta Kronlid, Andrea Needham, Jo Wilson and Angie Zelter had managed to disarm a Hawk fighter at British Aerospace Warton, Lancashire. The four women were, as consequence, being held in Risley Prison awaiting trial on serious charges. This Hawk was painted in Indonesian Air Force markings and had been due for delivery the following day to the genocidal Soeharto regime. How we were processing such information in the light of Scripture and inviting the broader St. Mary's parish into further non-violent resistance is exemplified in the following homily I gave at the Sunday masses before I departed to England.

'Today I have been asked to reflect on the reading from John Chapter 20 in the context of our past year at the Greg Shackleton Catholic Worker. Over the past few years it has become a real joy to break open the Scripture in community. Being raised a Catholic, I had developed immunity to Scripture by the time I had reached adulthood. The bible was boring, it's sole role being a cure for insomnia. The gospels seemed like four poorly written biographies, when one could have sufficed.

And anyway, the Protestants took the bible and we

took the sacraments, wasn't that the deal?

It took me a while to realise that the Scripture is great literature, heavily laden with cross references, so poetic, so alive, so layered; to be read in the company of others who are sharing the way, the path of discipleship. Serious reading of Scripture is a powerful interplay between the times of Jesus and the times of the discipleship community when the Scripture was written (in the case of John two generations later) and our time.

In his book entitled 'Who Will Roll Away the Stone? Discipleship Queries for First World Christians', Ched Meyers writes: 'In every age disciples despair that the story has ended, only to discover that the stone has been rolled away', reopening the possibility - and imperative - of following the way of Jesus. He then goes on to look at the spiritual and social stones that impede us, conversion as the second stage of discipleship and also reconstruction of the Church and the world. Our weekly bible study remains an important ingredient in our community's rhythm of action and reflection. Together with daily prayer and sacrament it remains ancient manna of desert travellers. Central to our faith is seeking an understanding of our historic moment and our responsibilities in it. This study was enlivened by the year spent in active solidarity with our brothers and sisters in East Timor. Their cries for justice continue to awaken and evangelise us.

In the next few days I will be travelling to England to attend the trial of a Catholic Worker friend Andrea Needham and three other women. In the early hours of January these four women made their way into a British Aerospace factory in northern England and with simple household hammers disarmed a Hawk Fighter being sold to the Indonesian dictatorship. These planes have been used to drop napalm and bomb villagers in the hills of East Timor.

Preceding tonight's reading it is Mary Magdalene - a woman - who recognises that Christ has risen. Like the four women in England there is recognition that life has conquered death, love triumphed over fear, that Jesus is risen. With this recognition what could be a more natural act, less criminal, than the disarmament of a hi-tech weapon system designed to bomb men, women and children in East Timor - after the twenty-year crucifixion of 200,000 East Timorese, the near genocide of a culture, the weapons dealing, the media management, the paralysis of good people. These four women in England sensed resurrection. They have seen that the imperial seal placed on the tomb of Jesus, placed on the fate of the people of East Timor and us all has been broken. An imperial seal placed by Rome, by Caesar, by Soeharto, by British Aerospace, by our government has been broken. Jesus has risen. A human response to these high crimes is in reach.

Unlike Simon Peter and John, in John 20:10, Mary and these women don't merely 'go home again'. Like Mary Magdalene they wait, weep, see and believe in a resurrection. After rolling away the roller door of the hangar, they carry out three million pounds of disarmament with simple household hammers. They stick photographs of East Timorese people to the plane. They sing. They cry. They dance. They hug. They go outside and dance under the security cameras. Like Mary they wish to share the good news. They phone from the hangar. They phone friends. They phone media. They phone British Aerospace. Their friends phone me - my heart leaps! Like with Mary there is general disbelief, there are handcuffs, criminal charges, no bail and jail. There is cynicism and apathy. There is disbelief, a recurring theme in today's reading

'On the evening of that day, the first day after the Sabbath, the doors were locked where the disciples were, because of their fear of the Judeans, but Jesus came and stood among them.' John 20:19

The response to Mary's news of resurrection is a negative evaluation, the doors are locked. In our context, we

41

as white Australians have been provided a protective bubble for the price of our silence. A bubble, or locked room, wherein we can live out our lives immune to the realities of our East Timorese, Bougainvillean and West Papuan brothers and sisters to the north. Military realities that facilitate the corporate armed robberies of oil from the Timor Sea, gold from the West Papuan highlands and copper from the island of Bougainville. Robberies that leave in their wake dead people, polluted waters, destroyed societies and cultures. The good news is that the apostles have remained together even in a paralysed state. This is enough to evoke an experience that is their salvation. We find Jesus in community.

'He said to them, 'Peace be with you' then he showed them his hands and his side. The disciples kept looking at the Lord and were full of joy. Again Jesus said to them, 'Peace be with you. As the Father has sent me so I am sending you. After saying this he breathed on them and said to them, 'Receive the Holy Spirit; for those who sins you forgive, they are forgiven; for those whose sins you retain, are retained.' John 20:20-23

Here Jesus gives two gifts, a commission and an admonishment. The commission makes community an imperative; the gifts of peace and the Holy Spirit and the admonishment to forgive makes community possible.

As Brazilian Bishop Helda Camara warns, Jesus does not offer the peace of a fermented swamp, the peace of the status quo resting on an underbelly of corruption and injustice. There are only two other references to peace in John's gospel and they are both couched in the assumption of persecution: In John 14:27: 'Peace be with you I give you my peace. Not as the world gives peace do I give to you. Do not be troubled. Do not be afraid.'

In John 16:33 'I have told you all this, so that in me you may have peace even though you have trouble in the world. Courage I have overcome the world.'

The commission is specific - the community is now the body of Christ in the world. As he has been sent he is now sending them. There is no distinction between Jesus and the community of believers in terms of divine mandate. What he began they (and we) must continue,
· to witness to God's love in the world
· to shed light on deed's done in darkness to convert them to acts of light

The admonishment to acknowledge sin and forgive each other is basic. As we have all painfully learnt; no forgiveness - no community.

The consequences of this commission stands before John's community in the person of the crucified Christ. John's community faces the impending violence of both Judea and Rome, water and blood flowed from Jesus side in a powerful imagery of birth. The way of the cross remains the path of discipleship. In East Timor, West Papua and Bougainville there are new corporate and imperial entities that secure wealth and power with the sword and helicopter gun ships. Many of these corporations and governments have offices in Brisbane; like Rome they threaten the cross that we, as disciples, embrace.

'Thomas, the twin, one of the twelve, was not with them when Jesus came. The other disciples told him, "We have seen the Lord", but he replied, "Until I have seen in his hands the print of the nails, and put my finger in the mark of the nails and my hand in his side, I will not believe."' John 20:24-25

This is hardly a surprising response from Thomas, we have met him twice already in John's gospel story. He is not a big fan of the way of the cross. In chapter 11 he responds to Jesus intention to risk going back into hostile Judea to rescue Lazarus with a brash and sarcastic suggestion, 'Let us all go back so we may die with him.'

In chapter 14, during the last supper Thomas has disclaimed either knowing where Jesus was going or 'the

43

Way'. A dead and buried Jesus has been a disappointment for Thomas in terms of Messianic hopes, but allows him to deny any implications about Jesus death for his own future. He really doesn't want to know about a resurrection. Maybe he has been absent checking out other career opportunities for a redundant disciple? Thomas demands proof that he believes is impossible to deliver. He embraces a state of unbelief.

'Eight days later, the disciples were in the house again and Thomas was with them. Despite the locked doors Jesus came in. He stood among them and said, "Peace be with you'. Then he said to Thomas, "Put your finger here and see my hands, stretch out you hand and put it into my side. Doubt no longer but believe."' John 20:26-27

It has been eight days since the disciples have experienced the resurrection and still the doors are locked. In our locked room we have been reduced to a state of virtual morality. Similar to the latest hi- tech entertainment sweeping the US that provides virtual reality - all the sensations of experience, without the experience.

The present analogy is a church and new age cousins that push a private salvation in the midst of a broad moral disintegration. The mushrooming of positive thinking groups amidst social cynicism and political impotence is one sign of this locked room. In the locked room we are reduced to a high drama/low reality discipleship that abandons our commission in a world that is literally dying to hear from us. A living faith must leave the locked room and open its heart to social and political reality.

'Thomas then said, "You are my Lord and my God" Jesus replied, "You believe because you see me, don't you? Happy are those who believe although they don't see."' John 20:28-29

Wes Howard Brooks sees this declaration by Thomas as the most joyous of John's gospel. It displays the emotional depth of the moment of conversion. One can picture Thomas the cynic, Thomas the sceptic we met in earlier chapters and has appeared as a more hardened version in this one - having his anger and disappointment washed away in tears of joy with his experience of the risen one. Thomas' statement, 'You are my Lord and my God' is not a statement of dogma, but of relationship. It is an illegal and treasonous statement, 'Lord and God' being a title given to Domitian, the Roman emperor at the time of writing of this gospel.

This incident deals with the states of belief and unbelief - both options of free will. It does not deal with proof; there will never be enough proof that cannot be subjected to further doubt. That is to say: we are created in the image of God, Jesus is the human one. Let's follow Him!

# 2 Britain

## 2.1 Seeds of Hope Ploughshares

I arrived in London in time for the 1996 British Aerospace AGM held at the Queen Elizabeth II conference centre in Westminster, the most secure venue in Europe.

Peace activists had managed to organise the purchase of single shares in BAe and gained entry to the AGM. As I vigilled outside the convention centre the various elements of the British peace movement came tumbling out on to the street having been evicted for interrupting the death-dealing proceedings inside. There were older women in sensible shoes, dread-locked eco-warriors, feminists in docs, church folks in collars and crucifixes, a wonderful sight. It was here that I met up with ploughshare activist Chris Coles.

Following our release from prison in the US, the FBI was kind enough to return our hammers and wire clippers. In the spirit of recycling we had sent a set to Chris in England. In January 1993 he walked into a British Aerospace factory in Stevenhenge, Herts. He was wearing a white lab coat with 'British Aerospace Bomb Disposal' written on the back, and carried a British Aerospace identity card stating 'Chris Coles: Disarmer'.

Over the next hour Chris visited four buildings causing over £150,000 worth of disarmament to military equipment destined for the war on East Timor. In court he invoked the Criminal Law Act of

1967 to argue that he was acting with reasonable force to prevent a crime, namely genocide. Unusually, the Judge instructed the jury to use their conscience, common sense and common humanity in reaching a verdict. 'If what Mr Coles says is happening in East Timor', he said, 'it may amount to genocide, which is a crime under British and international law.'

There was a hung jury and a second trial resulting in Chris receiving an eight-month prison sentence. Since Chris's ploughshare action, hundreds of people had taken part in civil disobedience at BAe sites in Stevenage, Brough and Warton ranging from symbolic fence cutting and seed-planting to roof-top occupations. In response, BAe had spent literally millions of pounds on increased security, infiltration and legal manoeuvres.

Following the BAe conference I hooked up with Stephen Hancock a ploughshares activist, who along with Mike Hutchinsen, had carried out the first disarmament action in Britain in 1990 on a US F1-11 stationed at Upper Heyford. The pair had worn Mickey Mouse ears during the operation, believing the US guards would not open fire on a silhouette of their icon. In 1990, they managed to perform one million pounds worth of disarmament to the cockpit, received six months jail and escaped unscathed. We were joined by three US ploughshares activists - Elmer Maas of the original Plowshares Eight group which had kicked off the movement with their 1980 disarmament of an MX missile nose cone at a Pennsylvania General Electric factory; Art Laffin who had carried out a couple of disarmament actions on the huge nuclear Trident submarines under construction in Connecticut; and Lyn Fredriksonn who had been recently released after serving a year for disarming an F-15E.

We jumped a train and travelled north to visit the 'Seeds of Hope' women in Risley prison. The gathering in the visiting room of Risley was a joyous collision of sixteen years of Ploughshare communities with this the 56th incarcerated community that had disarmed in the spirit of Isaiah.

Angie, Andrea, Jo and Lotta beamed with life, hope and resolve. They spoke of the night of disarmament, the present

47

realities of prison, the war on East Timor and the future trial hovering on the horizon. We were able to bring messages of solidarity and love from Australia, US, East Timor and West Papua. They had been denied bail and classified as high security prisoners by the Home Office.

I had met Andrea Needham in Washington DC. She was a qualified physiotherapist and was working with the homeless. She had attended our trial in Syracuse, New York, and in the meantime had returned to England where she had trained as a nurse and pursued serious non-violent resistance to the war machine. Jo Wilson was a tutor in further education and a borough councillor in Kirkby, a low-income area near Liverpool. Lotta Kronlid from Sweden was working as a gardener in Oxford. Angie Zelter from the Norfolk coast was a long-standing peace and environmental activist who had been imprisoned in Malaysia. The women had spent a year in preparation for the action along with six other women in an affinity group with various roles. This action was informed by a feminist critique of the war machine and of the peace/ploughshares movement. The group also had a strong emphasis on their disarmament being fully justified by international and British law. Three of them had carried out the act on January 29, while Angie appeared the next day at Norwich Magistrates Court to initiate legal action and announce that she would be carrying out a second disarmament action on the Hawk. Angie was arrested a week later on her way to British Aerospace Warton, hammer in hand.

On the pilot seat in the cockpit of the disarmed Hawk the women had left a video report containing eyewitness accounts of Hawks on bombing raids in East Timor; they further contained the personal statements of intent from all four women to disarm the Hawks bound for Indonesia. It was hoped that the video could be introduced as evidence in any consequent trial.

Since their arrest they had been joined by a legal team headed by Gareth Pierce, who had helped free the Guilford Four and the Birmingham Six.

The following day we four foreigners gathered outside a

48

windswept Crown Court in Preston, five miles from the BAe Warton factory. We held banners that read 'You Can Jail the Resister But Not the Resistance!' and 'Disarmament is a Duty Not a Crime!' We managed to get into the public gallery as the four women appeared for a pre-trial hearing. At this hearing the women secured a change of venue to Liverpool due to the dominance of British Aerospace in the Preston economy.

The following week we all headed to an international Ploughshares gathering at Basisgemeinde Wulfshagenerhutten, a rural community in northern Germany. Ploughshare activists from England, Holland, Germany and Sweden gathered for a week of reflection, celebration and conspiracy. Between those gathered, we had disarmed Trident submarines, F-15 and F1-11 fighter-bombers, B-52 Bomber, Pershing 11 Missiles, JAS attack plane, grenade launcher and an AK-5 automatic rifle. It was quite a swap meet. Basisgemeinde provided a wonderful setting for the gathering with its seventy intentional community members, many children and street people gathered around a rhythm of prayer, celebration and work in the self managed toy making factory and fields. Meanwhile the streets of Germany were experiencing the largest police mobilisation since the Nazi period as the government attempted to suppress mass opposition to its transporting of nuclear waste.

At the gathering we heard from some of the women in the Seeds of Hope affinity group. They had been doing a wonderful job in spreading the word, nationally and internationally, about the action and setting up support infrastructure for the imprisoned women. As the affinity group was London based, there was a need for local organising in Liverpool, the site of the forthcoming July trial. I decided to head there and see if I could offer some of my experience from organising around ploughshares trials in the US and solidarity actions around East Timor in Australia.

## 2.2 *Ploughshares Trial*

In Liverpool I was introduced to Terry Egan, a Trade Union activist, and Fr. Fitzgerald, a sympathetic Catholic priest, with an interest in social justice. I was given a room at St. Michael's Church and a phone and desk at the downtown Trade Union Centre and began to vigil daily outside the Liverpool Crown Courts. Over the six weeks of pre-trial local organising we managed to address and mobilise four local church communities. These folks were to provide the numbers on the streets and the hospitality for people coming from out of town. Our intention was to invite as many people as possible into the drama of the forthcoming trial. We spoke to churches, schools, Trade Unionists, an enclosed order of Carmelite nuns, peace activists, and a *L'Arche* community of adults with disabilities. For many, this was the first they had heard of East Timor and British arms sales to the Indonesian dictatorship.

A week before the trial was to begin, 100 local people celebrated a liturgy outside the court. It was the 20th anniversary of the annexation of East Timor by Indonesia. We were joined by Maureen Tolfree, a sister of English born Brian Peters who was one of the five Australian based journalists massacred by a raiding party of Indonesian troops at Balibo, East Timor, in October 1975.

With the four women and their legal team working on the court scene, the Seeds of Hope affinity group focussed on media and building national and international support. Our focus was on local organising and the street scene outside the trial.

In our literature we pushed a theme of celebration. The victory had been won, the Hawk disarmed. Hawk Jet ZH 955 was no longer going to Indonesia. Soeharto had rejected it demanding a replacement. Liverpool is a generally sympathetic town with a strong tradition of working class resistance. The local Dockers were in the middle of a protracted strike that commanded popular support. People in the street were receptive to our message as we distributed 20,000 leaflets in the six weeks leading up to the trial.

Our planned events were advertised under the banner 'GIVE PEACE A DANCE! in solidarity with the people of East Timor and the women on trial for disarming the Hawk.' In the week preceding the trial, a local feminist band, 'The Frocks', played a benefit gig for imprisoned women at the Trade Union Centre. On the eve of the trial we had planned a 'Celebration of Hope and Resistance' at St. Michael's social club, with cabaret, speeches and poetry where locals and out-of-towners were introduced for the week ahead. The night progressed with the sporadic arrival of Swedish backpackers at the end of a long hitch. On the Thursday night of the trial we planned a 'Ceilidh for Peace' with local band 'The Firkins' at the Irish Centre. This was followed by a rave at the Mardi Gras organised by young people in the dance scene. All these events at Left, Church, Irish and club venues were supported beyond our expectations and this support was reflected in the numbers in the streets and the word getting around town.

St. Lukes, the burnt out shell of a downtown church destroyed by German bombardment during the blitz, supplied an authentic starting point for the daily procession to the Crown Court. It made a clear connection between the historical suffering of Liverpool and East Timorese communities and the Hawk sales to the Indonesian dictatorship. At the beginning of each trial day we were addressed by a Liverpool Blitz survivor to the nature of aerial bombardment. Typical of these was Joe O'Grady, 69, from Walton, 'We lost our house five days before Christmas in the Blitz. As a survivor I know the horror being felt by the people of East Timor. Aerial bombardment makes you feel so helpless. We should not be profiting from the slaughter of innocents.'

On the eve of the trial the church leaders on Merseyside appealed to the British Government to stop exporting Hawk aircrafts to Indonesia while that country continued the illegal occupation of East Timor. The statement continued, 'We do not believe that British workers can rest easy if it becomes clears that their products and profits contribute to the oppression of defenceless people, or that we, in effect, condone occupation through military cooperation with the Indonesian Government.'

The letter to Prime Minister Major was signed by Roman Catholic Archbishop Patrick Kelly, the Free Church Moderator and the Anglican Bishop David Sheppard.

Each morning of the trial, over a hundred people would gather at St. Luke's dressed in black with the name of an East Timorese victim of Western weapons hanging around their neck. We would process down the main street to the sound of a drumbeat from a Buddhist monk and on occasion a lone piper.

As we arrived at the Crown Court we would build a makeshift shrine to the East Timorese dead and form a large circle holding hands. We would call out the names of the East Timorese dead and respond in chorus *Presente*. Such a solemn ritual set a serious tone and focus for folks joining us for the first time and members of the jury arriving for the day. Each day we would have fresh speakers, some of whom would offer their testimony at trial, some who had travelled internationally to show their solidarity, family members of the defendants and welcoming locals. A roster for the public gallery would be established along with a day-long vigil lead by the meditation drumming of a Buddhist nun. A Catholic mass was celebrated outside the court along with a variety of liturgical traditions during the week.

On the second night of the trial we hosted a packed public meeting at the Quaker Centre addressed by East Timorese leader José Ramos-Horta, Pax Christi's Pat Gafney who had recently returned from East Timor after delivering the ploughshares women's video, Carmel Budiardjo who had served three years as a political prisoner of Soeharto, and Emma from the 'Seeds of Hope' affinity group.

Ramos-Horta congratulated the women on trial stating, 'In twenty years of resistance, we were never able to shoot down an aircraft. You grounded one without firing a single shot and without hurting the pilot.'

In the prosecution's case, the videotape left in the cockpit was introduced as evidence of conspiracy, as it showed the four women explaining their intentions before the action. The video also showed evidence of genocide, with scenes of Indonesian soldiers murdering unarmed East Timorese. The tape ended with a plea by an East Timorese woman, 'Please stop your arms trade with Indonesia if you are really human.' As this video ended, the jury were clearly moved.

The defendants did not challenge the facts but cross examined some prosecution witnesses to tease out the issues. British Aerospace site manager at Warton, Christopher Foster, testified that the Hawk was primarily a training aircraft and he was confident that it could not take part in genocide. Cross-examined by Andrea, he admitted that the 'trainer' could carry anti-personnel cluster bombs.[4]

'Did you', she asked, 'have any concern for the people who might be killed when it was delivered?'

'No,' he replied, ' I had no concern.'

The judge accepted legal argument by Barrister Vera Baird, representing Jo, that justified calling expert witnesses in relation to the situation in East Timor. José Ramos-Horta recalled numerous instances of Hawks bombing villages. 'They are a constant threat to us,' he said, 'and we fear their supply.'

Paul Rogers, Professor of Peace Studies at Bradford University, testified that Hawks were an integral part of the Indonesian Air Force's 'Bandung Squadron', which was dedicated to counter-insurgency, which meant crushing the East Timorese resistance. He said the Hawks were designed to fly low and bomb undefended or lightly defended targets.

Carmel Budiardjo, the founder of Tapol, (an Indonesian human rights organisation) and a former political prisoner of the Indonesians described the years she and her husband, an Indonesian, were locked away by Soeharto without trial.

She outlined Tapol's documentation of the crimes of the

regime. John Pilger, expatriate Australian journalist and maker of the 'Death of a Nation' documentary, told of his clandestine visits to East Timor and the evidence of genocide that he collected.

The four women gave powerful testimony to how they had felt a moral and legal obligation to disarm the British Aerospace Hawk days from delivery to the genocidal Soeharto dictatorship for its war on the people of East Timor.

Vera Baird, the defence counsel, summed up with a simple analogy, 'Imagine if a person slashes the tyres of a car', she said. 'Under normal circumstances that would be a crime. But suppose they knew the car was carrying a bomb which would devastate Manchester city centre? (The massive IRA bombing of nearby Manchester a month before was fresh in the public mind.) In that case, slashing the tyres would not be a crime it would be a responsible and public-spirited act.'

The jury was initially out for four hours, before returning to announce they could not reach a unanimous decision. The judge said he would accept a majority decision of 10-2 or 11-1.

The jury returned to deliver verdicts of 'not guilty' on all seven charges of conspiracy and criminal damage. The court room erupted in celebration, a celebration that spread down the stairwells and elevators into the courtyard as scousers, nuns, punks and pagans danced wildly. The crowd of supporters were joined by the four defendants taking their first steps out of custody in six months. They were met by an astonished press pack that had up to that point largely ignored the case. Celebrations went on through the night at the Irish Centre.

The media blizzard of the verdict carried the word around the world. Responses to this, the first acquittal in the sixteen year history of the ploughshares movement, ranged from celebration in the mountains of East Timor and dissident jail cells of the US to calls for the abolition of the jury system by some enraged government MPs and the immediate issuing of civil injunctions by BAe on the four acquitted women.

## 2.3 An Experiment in Community, Hospitality and Resistance

Following the experiences of being awakened to British complicity in the genocide in East Timor and of faith-based solidarity around the ploughshares trial, local people asked me to stay in Liverpool and continue to explore Catholic Worker and Ploughshare themes. To continue the momentum from the trial we set a date for further resistance in mid-September. We would return to plant seeds of hope at British Aerospace Warton, where another twenty-four Hawks were on the production line for the Soeharto dictatorship.

St. Michael's parish gave us the use of a seven bedroom presbytery to the newly forming Liverpool Catholic Worker which provided great space for an 'intentional community' and the ability to host public meetings and provide accommodation for resistance gatherings. My intentions were to stay and help a local group get a Catholic Worker community off the ground and continue non-violent resistance with the praxis we had used in Australia which had been borrowed from the US Catholic Worker tradition of intentional community and faith based resistance. This praxis was relatively new to the English scene. As in Australia, Christian energy had been co-opted into the secular paradigms of the Labor Party and social work - managing dissent and managing the poor.

Given the lack of tradition, resources and local folks willing to move in and live in community we did pretty well over the next two years.

The intentional community was assembled by the end of 1996 consisting of Lizzie Jones coming from Wales, Treena Lenthall from a year with Catholic Worker communities in the U.S. and Annie Harrison returning from Germany. Our most solid support came from several working class families in the parish - Egans, Rudkins, Laings and Josie McFaralane. We would meet together on Sunday nights for bible study using Ched Meyers commentary on Mark's Gospel 'Binding the Strong Man' and planning hospitality and resistance projects.

These projects were firmly grounded in reality with the arrival of East Timorese exiles who had occupied embassies in Jakarta, had received asylum in Portugal and had come to Liverpool to join the campaign against the war on their people.

We were also nourished by the close proximity of the L'Arche community and visits from US ploughshare activists Art Laffin, Fr. John Dear, Fr. Frank Cordaro, Teresa Grady, and Kathy Kelly.

In our continued resistance organising we borrowed a model from the US of Faith and Resistance retreats, where participants would arrive in Liverpool for a day or two of reflection, community building, non-violence training and an evening of celebration. We would then drive an hour to British Aerospace Warton, with the action group going over the fence for an act of civil disobedience and the larger support group closing down the front gates in a solidarity ritual.

Many variations on the theme were brought to this formula by participants' cultures, faith traditions, personal experiences, organised political and theological presentations and artistic statement.

In this manner we were able to harness the energy of the ploughshares trial and acquittal to confront BAe Warton six times with civil disobedience over the next 18 months.

During this period when other aspects of the national anti-Hawk campaign were collapsing in exhaustion we were able to provide energy, organising and non-violent confrontation with the export deal.

The solidarity activism for East Timor attracted many visitors to Liverpool including José Ramos-Horta, Bishop Belo, Fr. Domingos Soares, Max Stahl, Andrew McNaughtan, Tom Hyland, Shirley Shackleton, Maureen Tolfree, Malcolm Rennie's mother, three members of Brisbane's Greg Shackleton Catholic Worker and numerous exiled East Timorese who found the Catholic Worker house a welcome place of hospitality, solidarity and celebration. We also offered short-term hospitality to families visiting Irish prisoners in jail in Liverpool. We reached out in solidarity with other prisoners and campaigns. We ran successful speaking series exploring the themes we were experimenting with in greater depth. It was an intense experiment with radical discipleship in a society that reaps the benefits of global violence and theft.

As Meyers reflects on the Last Supper discourse, community is an experience of intimacy and betrayal and ours did not disappoint in this regard. In a similar two-year lifespan and conclusion to the Greg Shackleton House experiment it was to end with an eviction by the Church establishment and much shaking of sand from the feet. As an experiment, no participant doubted its significance in shaking and waking them from their First World slumber. Questions may still remain on how transportable Catholic Worker is from its American context and how sensible a landlord/tenant relationship is with the church bureaucracy.

## 2.4 *Vines, Fig Trees and a Special Branch*

In mid-September 1996 over forty people including the recently acquitted Jo and Andrea and Max Stahl, the cameraperson who had filmed the massacre at the Santa Cruz cemetery, gathered for our first return to the site. Following a multi-faith service at the main gates, a convoy was formed which wound its way round from the north of the factory to the runway's east end. Police vehicles were blocked and Maggie Egan, a school teacher from Liverpool, Stephen Hancock, a peace activist from Oxford; Irfan Merchant, a trainee doctor from Edinburgh, James, a Liverpool High School student and I used a three person human staircase to climb over the wooden perimeter fence and gain access to the BAe site. Supporters unfurled a banner reading 'Don't Export Death to the Children of East Timor.'

We then proceeded to plant a variety of seeds in an attempt to enflesh the prophecy of Micah, who talks of a time when 'everyone shall sit underneath their vine and fig-tree, and none shall make them afraid.' We were arrested and taken to Preston police station and offered cautions. Stephen and I refused and were held for another five hours and charged with 'trespass on an aerodrome.' Stephen Hancock's official statement to the desk sergeant read, 'We look forward to the day when BAe Warton is no longer used for the production of Hawk warplanes and other murderous weapons, but instead overgrown with trees, crops and vegetable plots.'

As we were going on the offensive, so was the State. The Lancashire Special Branch had approached Janet Lovelace, a former policewoman, with a proposition to infiltrate our organisation.

'They offered me 200 pounds a month, plus expenses and a bonus, if I came up with good information. They wanted names and anyone doing the organising. They said any domestic worries you have, any bills you have, don't worry, we will sort them out for you. If I got arrested they would sort that out for me. The 200 pounds was for the first three months, then it might be upgraded. They also offered me a mobile telephone, petrol and child-minding fees. All of it was to be paid in cash and the taxman need never know about it. They said no one need ever know about it.' (*The Guardian* September 1996)

Her first requested assignment was to attend the Ceilidh at the Liverpool Irish Centre that we had organised to kick off our weekend of faith and resistance. Janet Lovelace, a woman of exceptional integrity and courage, went to *The Guardian* newspaper who wired her up and returned for a second meeting with the Special Branch officers. The exposé on the second page of this national newspaper did not seem to embarrass the Special Branch who declared it normal policing policy. It was clear that the judiciary and police had not taken up the message implicit in the Liverpool jury's verdict and had begun a further inquiry into allegations of BAe's complicity in genocide. Instead they had chosen to expend resources to investigate the messengers. What was also informative concerning the relationship between State and corporate power was that BAe knew that this particular approach to Janet Lovelace was being made by Special Branch.

BAe also moved rapidly. Two days after our arrest Stephen and I received phone calls from Freshfields and Associates informing us that they would be taking out temporary injunctions on us in the High Court the following day.

Stephen got down to the High Court to witness the injunction process in the Judges' chambers and attempted to scribble down what they meant.

The terms within the injunction not only forbade the activists to trespass on or blockade BAe sites, but also forbade them to, 'Cause, assist, counsel, procure or incite their servants or agents or otherwise, whether directly or indirectly to do such things.' It cut heavily into free speech. It raised the stakes to a possible two years imprisonment for acts that may not have been punishable under criminal law. We knew of their power as Chris Coles, restrained by a similar injunction in 1994 had already been sentenced for 'contempt of court' to six months, merely for writing a leaflet encouraging people to blockade BAe. Evidence against him had been supplied by private detectives hired to attend public meetings he had addressed. Our case brought to thirteen the number of non-violent activists injuncted by Bae; Chris Coles, Mil Rai, the four ploughshares women, Jon Stoker, Faith Kenrick, Clive Fudge and the four most recent injunctees, Michael Bane Stuart Cooper, Stephen and myself.

Freshfields offered injunctees a deal (or a threat) that if they agreed to waiving a defence and making the injunctions permanent and lifelong, they in turn would waive costs, otherwise we would be looking at enormous court costs. Michael, Stuart, Stephen and I decided to go for broke and were set down for a hearing in the High Court on December 19 1996. Many of the other injunctees joined us in a vigil outside the court.

The contrast of resources assembled in the Judge's chambers was stunning. We four defendants walked in with our backpacks and sleeping bags after crashing on floor space in London the previous night. Freshfield's legal team, who also represent Rolls Royce in their Saudi arms dealings, glided in single minded, two-faced, three-piece suited, well-resourced and ready for action.

BAe's barrister argued that the various non-violent actions at BAe over the last four years, ranging from two ploughshare actions through several mass trespasses to symbolic trespasses and acts of fence-cutting, amounted to a concerted effort against BAe's business, that treating these actions through the criminal courts had not stopped the campaign, and that BAe deserved the protection of the High Court to forbid such actions.

Representing ourselves, we four defendants employed a variety of defences from legal, political, moral and religious perspectives. When it was pointed out that BAe's barrister hadn't challenged the defendants' assertion that crimes of genocide were being committed in East Timor, he replied that, 'We haven't condescended to detail about what is happening in East Timor because it is absolutely irrelevant.'

The Judge agreed with BAe, saying he thought there could be no legal defence to any non-violent resistance at BAe sites, that there was nothing to 'suggest that the conduct of the plaintiffs was in breach of the laws of this country', and that BAe was entitled to the protection of the court to prevent any further 'embarrassment.' Referring to the case of the four 'East Timor Ploughshares' women and their acquittal for disarming a Hawk, he said that this was an irrelevant case as it was not won at an appeal level and thus was not afforded the status of legal precedence under British law. He granted BAe the injunction and also granted them the right, if they so chose, to pursue the four defendants for court costs. This amounted to 100,000 pounds each for the afternoon.

During his defence, Stephen Hancock said that, 'Institutions often find it difficult to recognise massive crimes occurring under their own noses. We have a whole range of international treaties which testify to this inability. Today, we ask you to break this tradition, cast your glance wider, consider the plight of the people of East Timor and British Aerospace's complicity in their genocide, and to refuse to lend institutional legitimacy to an illegitimate, immoral and criminal business.'

After the case he noted that, 'The legal system has shown itself to be out of step with justice. This is sad but not surprising. As the weapons exports to Indonesia continue, so must our non-violent opposition.'

## 2.5  *Midwives, Magi and Us*

I f BAe thought that these injunctions would be the end of resistance to their Hawk deal with Indonesia they were wrong. Within the week, Stephen and I had decided to break them. We chose the Feast of the Holy Innocents that occurred a few days after Christmas. The feast recalls when King Herod, threatened by the birth of the Christ-child, attempted to maintain his power by ordering the slaughter of Jewish babies. We saw the clear link between this biblical story and the present day reality where those in power are prepared to sacrifice innocent civilians in an attempt to uphold their own political and economic interests.

We found good role models in the wise men, or magi, who were injuncted to return to Herod with news of the baby. We were injuncted to keep silent about the genocide in East Timor. Stephen and I were injuncted by the High Court. Margarita Egan, Anne Harrison, Mike Hutchinson, Treena Lenthall and Alan Thornton, who decided to join us in civil disobedience, were injuncted by the implicit threat of High Court action, the associated legal costs and prison sentences. Following the example of the magi who refused to cooperate with Herod's injunction and the midwives of the first chapter of Exodus who broke Pharaoh's injunction to kill Jewish newborn males, we too would break our injunction.

Our action followed a weekend Faith and Resistance retreat at the Liverpool Catholic Worker. The gathering was strengthened by the attendance of four other injunctees and five East Timorese exiles.

On Sunday December 29, eighty folks gathered at the entry to British Aerospace Warton for a liturgy of repentance, hope and resistance. During the liturgy, the BAe entry gate was decorated with scores of photos of children known and unknown to us. While the liturgy was in progress, we seven climbed the fence in another part of the factory. We carried a child's coffin containing pictures of East Timorese victims, copies of our High Court injunctions and other symbols. After gaining entry to the factory grounds we began a liturgy and started to dig a grave.

Our readings of the injunctions of the prophets Isaiah and Micah 'to beat swords into ploughshares and study war no more' were interrupted by BAe security who confiscated our shovel and detained us after we refused to leave the grounds. We were handed over to the police who charged us all with 'trespass on an aerodrome'. Stephen and I were held overnight while the others were released.

We all received a magistrates hearing date for April, but Stephen and I were set down for sentencing at the High Court in London on the civil matter in January. Such 'quick justice' is facilitated due to criminal cases requiring a burden 'to prove guilt beyond reasonable doubt' whereas with civil law merely 'the balance of probabilities' need suffice.

Given the sentence handed out previously to Chris Cole, Stephen and I packed our bags for a six-month stay. We had farewell parties in Liverpool and Oxford and rose before dawn to catch a bus to London with about twenty supporters. There was a great vibe in the bus, feeling like a football team playing away with little chance of short-term victory.

Outside the imposing architecture of the High Court there were about sixty folks gathered in solidarity, along with a heap of paparazzi photographers clicking and flashing away, a surreal feeling of being feted and fatted for the slaughter.

Inside, the layered authoritarian decor of the court was imposing. Behind us the gallery looked like the terraces from a feral football game with East Timorese faces, dreadlocks, and old, gentle faces beaming at us. The corporate legal team looked like the slick bad guys they are, as they presented their submissions requesting our imprisonment. We both spoke clearly. We asked the court to distinguish between legitimate 'property' which the law was designed to protect, and illegitimate 'contraband' which by law has no right to exist and should be confiscated. Instruments of war designed and intended for illegal purposes, such as genocide, would logically fall under the latter category, and therefore have no rights to be 'protected' by injunctions or any other legal measures.

The Judge replied, 'No-one can fail to be impressed by the sincerity of your convictions!' and imposed two suspended sentences of three months, saying it would be a sword of Damocles hanging over us.

We hadn't thought of this result. Our supporters thought it at least rated as an away draw against top-flight opposition. We exited the court and processed to Downing St., BAe offices, Rolls Royce offices and the Department of Trade and Industry with two van loads of riot police trailing us, delivering counter-injunctions against their war making.

Stephen reflected well on the nature of the sentence which he defined as suspended animation...

> 'A friend just wrote to me: "Bet you wished you had bought a return coach ticket." I must admit: I'm feeling both exhausted and disorientated. I had fully been expecting to be living with Ciaron in a north London prison cell. In his judgement, the judge made discernible noises about their being serious public issues at stake and that ours was not merely a case of groundless intrusion, but he made it quite clear that the injunction was legitimate, and that we had broken it. And then he proceeded to dangle, in his own words, 'a sword of Damocles' over our heads - in the form of a three months sentence, suspended for a year. A judicial shot across our bows - or even through our sails.
>
> Part of me smiled, part of me slumped. Relieved, because I'd been very anxious about going to prison.

Disappointed, because I had been prepared for prison, had invested a lot of energy and self in the process, and would now have to gear back down, before gearing back all over again.

As soon as the judge left, reporters started asking: Are you going to break it again? And I said, I'll have to see, but I could have been more honest and straightforward. I think my reluctance is a deep one - to admit to resistance being a requested rhythm of my life.

The Judge has sentenced us to a state of suspension.

What helped me to transform the tension of the whole injunction process into something less debilitating and more creative was experiencing it as an invitation - to clarification, to faithfulness towards my sisters and brothers in East Timor.

I will endeavour to experience this suspended sentence in a similar way.

Suspension is an accurate description of our state of existence. Very few of us are in prison for our beliefs and actions. But all of us are suspended in, and by fear - not quite daring to let our bodies follow our consciences. So, the judge has prescribed a very accurate sentence, in some ways more effective than prison.

What we need from judges and institutions of this country are not discernible noises, but unmistakably clear voices: we will neither tolerate nor legitimise British Aerospace aiding and abetting genocide in East Timor.

That demand is also made of ourselves, swords dangling over our heads. I can think of much better uses for swords!

As long as the Hawks fly and the people of East Timor live under fear, there is an open invitation to us all, for clear voices and actions, inside, outside, up and over the fences that divide our human family.'

Our open breaking of the injunctions broke the back of this BAe strategy. No one else was injuncted following this action.

However, the draconian injunctions were relatively effective for BAe, with many of those injuncted moving on to other aspects of the campaign or other campaigns entirely. For the Liverpool Catholic Worker our response called forth others from our growing network to take non-violent action at the British Aerospace factory and for a fresh focus on the Government's Department of Trade and Industry that issued the export licenses for weapons exports.

## 2.6 *Easter at Warton*

Over Easter 1997, fifty folks gathered in Liverpool for an Easter 'Faith and Resistance' retreat reflecting on the themes of crucifixion, waiting and resurrection in the context of Britain's contribution to the war on East Timor. At the Celebration of Hope on the Saturday night we were addressed by Jo Wilson of the Seeds of Hope Ploughshares community. We were also entertained by excerpts from a locally produced play 'A Hammer in the Hand' inspired by the Ploughshares trial and the war in East Timor. The weekend included reflections and non-violence training.

At 5.40 am on Easter Monday morning four English peace activists and four East Timorese exiles entered BAe Warton. Before their arrest they recited prayers, read from the Bible, scattered seeds of hope, unfurled a banner reading 'Resurrection is Resistance!' and offered Easter eggs to BAe security staff.

One of those arrested was Fr. Fitzgerald of St. Michael's parish. The arrest of a priest attracted national and local media attention. It also made a clear link with the church of East Timor where it continued to play the main role of opposition and non-violent resistance. Prior to the action Fr. Fitzgerald stated, 'I will be accompanying Costa and Lopes, who live with St Michael's Parish at the Catholic Worker community, over the Warton fence in order to celebrate Easter, to celebrate this manifestation of the resurrection, that these two men have survived the genocide and are here alive, among us. They ask of simple things; to repent of our complicity in the death of their nation - to end these weapon exports.'

Later that morning a liturgy was held by a hundred solidarity activists at the gates of BAe Warton. The gathering then joined two Buddhist monks holding vigil outside the nearby Lytham police station which held Fr. Fitzgerald, James Cookson, Lizzie Jones, Julie Currall, Moises da Costa, Kupa Lopes, Amorim Vieira, and Acaçio Marques. Acaçio had spent two years in prison in East Timor. The presence of East Timorese in non-violent resistance at a corporate site producing the weapons that were slaying their people was extremely powerful.

Months later the court case was enriched by the testimony of Max Stahl, who had filmed the Easter action and the Santa Cruz cemetery massacre six years before. Proceedings in Lytham magistrates were often drowned out by low flying Hawk aircraft taking off from nearby Warton. The East Timorese told the Court of their own personal sightings of Hawk jets above their homeland. They explained how jets were used to threaten as well as to bomb. Vieira told the court that in 1992 he was aboard a peace ship sailing from Darwin to East Timor to commemorate the first anniversary of the Díli massacre. It had to turn back after Hawk jets repeatedly circled it. Here were witnesses that had been personally threatened by Hawks on patrol in East Timor in a court whose government denied their use in the area. Six of the eight prosecution witnesses, including police and security guards, agreed that since the demonstrations began their knowledge of the issue had increased.

Before pronouncing sentence the magistrate twice told the court, packed with supporters: 'We have heard your message and taken it to heart.' The decision not to impose a fine underlined the court's comment. Reflecting on the magistrates words, Fr. Fitzgerald explained how his parish of St. Michael's had been evangelised by the East Timorese guests and now they were having the same effect on the British institution of Lytham Magistrates Court.

We had maintained a weekly vigil outside Warton throughout Lent leading up to the Easter witness, which continued on a monthly basis throughout the rest of the year. On the July 1997 anniversary of the Seeds of Hope Ploughshares acquittal, twenty-five folks from eight different countries joined us for a five-day, 45 mile walk from Liverpool Crown courts to BAe Warton. We offered reflection evenings with the various communities that offered us hospitality en route. We were joined at Lytham for the last three miles by fifty local people. On arrival at the gates of BAe Warton there was chanting from four Buddhist monks, bible readings and a litany for the dead of East Timor.

We then formed a circle while playing Sting's 'Message in a Bottle' over the boom box. We spread bottles, collected en route, over the entry to BAe containing messages of peace and disarmament in a variety of languages. Meanwhile, Kupa Lopes walked calmly to the sign bearing BAe's corporate logo. He delivered a powerful message from another bottle, throwing blood over the logo: 'BAe continues to spill the blood of East Timorese brothers and sisters'.

Kupa stated, 'The blood for this action was donated by a survivor of the Hawk bombardment of the Matebean Mountains. His relatives and friends were not so lucky. I saw the Hawks flying those missions; thousands of East Timorese have died because of British Aerospace Hawks. We call upon the British government to immediately stop the sale of Hawks to dictator Soeharto.'

## 2.7 Department of Terminal Indifference

Using the momentum following the acquittal and the resources of Campaign Against the Arms Trade, Angie Zelter and friends organised a week long non-violent siege of the Department of Trade and Industry (DTI) in London leading up to the 1996 anniversary of the December 7 Indonesian invasion of East Timor. Continuity of presence was provided by four Buddhist monks from Nipponzon Myohoji as student, peace and solidarity groups travelled to join the vigil.

Tom Hyland and four East Timorese living in Dublin came over and joined other English-based exiles in the weeklong demonstration. The Irish Campaign in solidarity with East Timor had been hugely successful in bringing the message to that country. The Irish President Mary Robinson was well briefed on East Timor by the time she became head of the UN human rights effort. Various celebrities and politicians joined and addressed the vigil throughout the week. Occupations and blockades of the DTI also took place.

Meanwhile, down at the Indonesian Embassy, US public relations giant Burson-Marsteller had been charged with the job of celebrating the Soeharto dictatorship and limiting the PR damage of the coming week's awarding of the Nobel Peace Prize to East Timorese dissidents, Bishop Belo and José Ramos-Horta.

They chose the eve of the anniversary of the invasion of East Timor to gather journalists for lunch, fine wine, distribution of presents and a detailed presentation at the Embassy. Guests entering the embassy were met by demonstrators. Lunch in the magnificent first-floor dining room was interrupted as four East Timorese and solidarity activists hauled themselves up to the Georgian balcony, yelling 'Free East Timor!' through the windows. Police and security guards pounded past the aperitif-gulping diners, dragging the protesters through the embassy. Twenty minutes on, the usually suave ambassador, Habibie, was still trying to contain his anger.

We soon discovered that Liverpool had its very own DTI Office in the Cunard Buildings down on the docks. Given that Britain is the world's second largest arms exporter with the Indonesian dictatorship buying a wide range of small arms, water cannon, armoured personnel carriers, tanks and Hawk ground-attack aircraft, we decided to kick off Lent 1997 with a visit. Following an Ash Wednesday liturgy in a downtown church, during which we burned government papers and marked each other with their ashes, we headed with thirty others to the DTI. Four of us, dressed as spectres of death, carried signs identifying specific weapons for which the DTI had issued permits to export to the Soeharto dictatorship of Indonesia. We began a repentance liturgy in the office disrupting work until evicted by the police.

On the 1997 anniversary of the annexation we decided to return with more resolve. We celebrated a downtown mass with radical priest Fr. Domingos Soares, known as 'Fr. Maubere' and in exile from East Timor. We recalled the twenty-two year war of aerial bombardment, mass infantry, torture, assassination, forced starvation and sterilisation. We recalled that on July 17 1976 the Indonesian dictatorship, formally, and criminally, annexed East Timor. We were accompanied by Natalim de Arajio Duarte whose father had spent the past eight years in an Indonesian prison.

As twenty-five folks entered the offices of the DTI, I poured human blood on one of the internal marble pillars while Kupa smeared another pillar with ash.

We were joined by Moises da Costa and Maureen Wallace in occupying the work area of the office bearing signs demanding the end of arms exports to Indonesia. Others occupied the customer

71

area and began a service around a banner that read 'Annexation Never; Solidarity Forever: Timor L'este Livre Now!' The service included readings of the names of East Timorese dead, testimonies from East Timor, and Scripture readings and songs in English and Tetum. The beautiful Cunard building offered great acoustics for US peace activist Teresa Grady who lead us in song. We stated,

'Today, we bring the symbols of blood and ash to the Department of Trade and Industry. Today is the 21st anniversary of Indonesia's annexation of East Timor. An annexation that remains unrecognised by the United Nations and universally condemned. An annexation that has transformed East Timor into killing fields of blood and ash - into a 'land of crosses.' An annexation made possible only by the weapons supplied from Britain, the US and Australia, weapons that have killed over a third of the East Timorese population.

Weapons sanctioned by the DTI for export to the Soeharto dictatorship provide for a military strategy of escalation dominance. The small automatic weapons manufactured by Royal Ordinance, maintain the daily grind of terror. Armoured personnel carriers and military land rovers deploy the occupying forces. The Glover-Webb water cannon is turned on demonstrations of the oppressed. The Alvis tanks are equipped to escalate the killing capacity of the Indonesian forces to the next level. If need be, as has been the case in the past, the British Aerospace Hawk ground attack aircraft is deployed to deliver death from the sky.

We come here today in a spirit of non-violent resistance to these high crimes of corporations and government departments. We come here today with survivors of the genocide unleashed on East Timor.

They awaken us to the deep spiritual danger we are in as a community complicit with genocide. We come here risking our liberty - to speak truth to power.'

After an hour of disrupting business as usual, police moved

in arresting Kupa and Costa for 'breach of the peace' and myself for 'criminal damage'. James Cookson was also arrested for refusing to vacate the building. The arresting officer was particularly rough, twisting the handcuffs, verbally abusing us in the vehicle and opening the watch house door with my face. At the watch house, three gigantic cops stood around Costa as he was processed. His contrasting slight build seemed a metaphor for what his people had been up against for so long.

At the end of September 1997 Foreign Secretary Robin Cook rejected the export licenses for a shipment of sniper rifles and personnel carriers bound for Indonesia. Could this be the first sign of the much vaunted 'ethical foreign policy' in relation to the Indonesian dictatorship? Or was it merely a piece of pre-Labour Party Conference tokenism?

In early October, in response to the rejection of the sniper rifles and APC permits we brought a basket of corn, rice, bananas, mangos and flowers (symbols of East Timorese life) to the DTI. We caught the security (which we discovered had been outfitted with thousands of pounds worth of hi-tech surveillance equipment since our July visit) on the hop with our non-violent fruit and veggie ram raid.

Most of our number accessed the office with a message of 'Continue to choose life; don't export death!' The rest of us occupied the foyer with song and testimony before continuing to vigil outside the building.

Britain continues to flood the killing fields of Indonesia, Africa and South America with many and varied weapons. Evidence of New Labour's ethical foreign policy has yet to surface.

## 2.8 Jailed Remembering the Dead

Throughout 1997, the activist East Timorese exile community was growing in England. Four young men were living in Dublin with some specific support from the Irish Government and operating in the context of a strong grassroots campaign of awareness raising and solidarity. East Timorese arriving in England were not, by and large, experiencing similar practical support from the more bureaucratic campaign organisations who were keen to use them for photo ops but provided little practical support.

The Catholic Worker network in Oxford, along with Stephen Hancock, offered help in finding accommodation and jobs. Fr. Paul Sanders in London began offering long term hospitality to a few of the exiles. The Liverpool Catholic Worker increasingly saw itself as a place for the East Timorese to land, spend six months in developing language skills, operate in the context of direct campaigning and move south where job and study opportunities were more plentiful.

Due largely to the warm hospitality of the extended community, strong familial relations developed and the Catholic Worker scene became a significant terms of reference for the exile community nationally, a place of gathering, celebration and action.

Strengthened by a growing sense of solidarity and urgency, the exiled activists chose the anniversary of the Díli massacre to act again at BAe Warton.

On the eve of the anniversary November 11 1997 about fifty folks gathered in the rain for a memorial service at the entrance to BAe Warton. Many of the East Timorese were survivors of other massacres from ground and air attack. Max Stahl gave an eyewitness account of the Santa Cruz cemetery massacre being recalled. Following the service, a dozen people kept vigil throughout the wet night sustained by the chanting and drum-beating of the Buddhist monks and recitation of the rosary.

At dawn at another part of the factory, Fr. Martin Newell, Roger Morby and Jan Harper joined six East Timorese in climbing the fence into BAe. They unfurled duplicate banners of those used at the Santa Cruz cemetery, one in broken English profoundly stating 'Independence is what we Inspire!' Following their arrest the East Timorese chose to increase the level of resistance by refusing to give their names.

The refusal was in solidarity with all the nameless dead of East Timor killed by British supplied weapons. By naming British Aerospace as complicit in the genocide of their people, and withholding their names, the six East Timorese were raising significant issues for us. Who are the criminals here? Are BAe Hawks trespassing over East Timor? The six were taken to Preston prison in what was a profound witness: that six people who were on the receiving end of our Hawks and guns in a faraway land were now here with us in our prisons for the act of non-violently remembering their dead.

In custody, court and jail the East Timorese remained resolutely nameless and were referred to as Number One, Number Two etc. Initially in Preston prison they received physical and verbal racial harassment. Most of the six could not speak English. We set up a daily vigil outside the prison and rostered on for visits. We were able to explain to other visitors what was going down and this improved their treatment on the inside. A week after their arrest they were taken to Lytham courts where they were told they would be granted bail if they gave their names. They refused and were returned to prison. We continued organising in Preston and spreading the word nationally and internationally.

After a second week they were once again taken back to Lytham. Their duty solicitor was obviously distressed. He told the magistrate that all his training would lead him to put in a bail application, but his clients had instructed him not to. He then explained to the magistrates why he believed they were taking this course of action. He spoke of the war in East Timor and how the British Government and British Aerospace were fuelling it. It was quite an impassioned speech from someone who had been drafted into the drama.

British Aerospace representatives and Special Branch conferred with the senior prosecutor from Blackpool who then amazingly put in a bail application on behalf of the nameless defendants he was supposed to be prosecuting. The duty solicitor exclaimed that having a prosecutor put in a bail application was legal history. The six East Timorese were cut loose having given no name or address. The duty solicitor then went on to invest himself in the case and months later made moves to summons the BAe management to testify what they knew about the genocide in East Timor. The charges were mysteriously dropped.

We were on a roll. Within fifteen months the situation had gone from BAe injuncting arrestees to stopping injuncting to not imposing fines, to dropping charges.

# 3　East Timor

## 3.1　Soeharto Falls, Stumbles or Shuffles Sideways?

We kick-started Lent 1998 with a vigil in downtown Preston and a twelve mile walk out to BAe Warton. By the time I left England another continuous Lenten witness was under way at the home of the Hawks. The charge over the fence at Easter would be lead by 80 year old blitz survivor Molly O'Connell.

As I arrived back in Australia, nineteen folks were facing trial for a trespass action at Canungra on the previous Invasion Day anniversary December 7. The action happened less than a week after nine people had appeared in court for the August 1997 arrests at the conclusion of a 'Journey for Peace'. In finding the nine guilty Beenleigh Magistrate Cheryl Cornack acknowledged, 'There are some people who hold moral beliefs so passionately that they are prepared to break the law to bring about social change. Many Australians are proud of criminal histories that show they have broken laws to bring about social change. And it is clear that protest is an important part of our community.'

During the December 7 civil disobedience, former army Major Terence Fisher burned his Defence Force commission after telling fellow protesters that Australian army trainers had 'blood on their hands' for helping hone the skills of Indonesian soldiers. While later being interviewed by mobile phone from his cell in the Beenleigh watch house he told a reporter that, 'those same soldiers would be used to brutally suppress the East Timorese independence movement. It's scandalous the way the current Australian Army carries on.'

Also among those arrested were Uniting Church Minister Noel Preston, Green Party Senate candidate Drew Hutton, former military chaplain and Roman Catholic priest Fr Peter Kennedy and East Timorese exile Afonso Corte Real.

The number of arrests, the variety of backgrounds of those arrested and the extensive media coverage indicated a growing awareness and concern in the Australian community over East Timor.

As the nineteen headed for court, events were moving rapidly in Jakarta. Preceded by several years of intense economic, ecological and political chaos, the aging General Soeharto found himself sandwiched between huge student-led demonstrations on the streets and enormous pressure from the International Monetary Fund to impose unpopular structural adjustments. The CIA backed General had been brought to power thirty years earlier with the mass extermination of leftists and others in 1964-65 - over one million killed and 750,000 imprisoned.[5]

So strategically significant to the US was the overthrow of the non-aligned Soekarno, Soeharto's provision of a 'stable investment climate' for Western corporations and the holocaust of any political opposition, that Robert McNamara later reflected the US should have withdrawn from the Vietnam War with Southeast Asia secured by this development.

Soeharto headed a system of entrenched and pervasive military corruption. More so than anywhere else in the world, the Indonesian Generals used political power to catapult themselves to élite economic status.

From the ritualised retail bribes to the wholesale military control of State enterprises and embezzlement of international aid, the Generals had for three decades plundered and mismanaged an economy that had become increasingly sophisticated. Those who really called the shots, those in suits with offices in DC and New York, had decided that Generals were too inefficient, that their time was over.

Sections of the Indonesian military who had reaped wealth from the thirty year arrangement throughout the archipelago and in East Timor did not plan to relinquish power and privilege quietly.

During the chaos of April 1998, as demonstrations turned to large-scale riots and loss of life, Soeharto's son-in-law and commander of Kopassus, Lieutenant-General Prabowo Subianto, made initial coup moves. These moves were unsuccessful. General Wiranto emerged as powerbroker and Prabowo was initially demoted to an academic post and eventually fled the country finding asylum in Jordan.

General Wiranto oversaw the live telecast theatre of the transition of power to Vice President Habibie with guarantees that Soeharto would be immune from prosecution in relation to his thirty-year rule. The theatre of exit of the General Soeharto and ushering in of the technocrat Habibie was deeply symbolic of the Western agenda for Indonesia.

## 3.2 Dwelling in Darwin

In the May of 1998, Treena Lenthall and I formed a ploughshares community with the intention of disabling uranium-mining equipment at the new Jabiluka mine site in the Northern Territory. Although both of us had been involved in several years of activism against the war in East Timor, we felt it important to address Australia's contribution to the nuclear war machine. This urgency had increased with the use of Depleted Uranium (DU) munitions in the Gulf Massacre and their consequent proliferation. During the 1991 Gulf Massacre UK and US forces fired over 14,000 11 lb. DU shells and over one million 1/2 lb DU bullets leaving battlefields radioactive and the rates of cancer and leukaemia soaring among Iraqi civilians.

In June, we joined a busload of activists for the 2,000-mile journey to the blockade of the mine site located in the wilderness of Kakadu, Northern Territory.

On the anniversary of Nagasaki Day (August 9 1998) we managed to disable a huge excavator at the Jabiluka mine after pouring blood, hammering its dashboard and cutting internal cables. We spent two months in Darwin Jail on remand and another two months out on bail in Darwin awaiting our court case.

The endless bus ride north was instructive on how huge Australia is, Brisbane being the closest capital city to Darwin 2,000 miles away.

East Timor may only be 300 miles from Darwin, but the tyranny of distance (in Australia, we are far from each other and far from the rest of the world) has played into an 'outta sight/outta mind' attitude mitigating against building resistance to the twenty-four year war in this neighbouring country. The distance between cities makes it very difficult to organise against the national government and military.

Life and politics outside the Sydney-Canberra-Melbourne loop is doomed to be relatively parochial. Darwin with a 60,000 population in the Northern Territory of 180,000 people is an extreme example of this phenomenon. Sydney and Melbourne, where the largest communities of East Timorese exiles are based, are 2,500 to 3,000 miles to the south.

Darwin is certainly interesting. It is probably the least Anglo town in Australia, with large indigenous and Asian communities. East Timorese make up roughly 8% of the population. It has a huge Indonesian Consul building downtown and an expensive Soeharto yacht anchored offshore. It was home to a small hardcore of Australian East Timorese activists who have kept posing the questions over the years with solidarity and direct action, targeting the consul, Department of Foreign Affairs, military training and visiting Indonesian and Australian Government bureaucrats. These people became our primary support in the second half of 1998 as we were released on bail and awaited our court case.

While on bail, we moved into a house of East Timorese solidarity activists. It was becoming apparent that there was movement in East Timor with the advent of the new Habibie administration. A number of political prisoners had been freed and there was talk of the first Indonesian election not rigged by Soeharto and the Golkar Party in thirty long years.

There was a lot more coming and going between Darwin and Díli. A group of East Timorese students visited the Jabiluka blockade before returning to Díli. They were upbeat about prospects for change. A number of folks from the blockade went on to East Timor.

Crashing at the house was John Martinkus, a young

81

Australian journalist writing for *The Sydney Morning Herald*. John had been investigating the October 1975 Balibo Massacre and had made the link with the present Indonesian Minister for Information, Yunus Yosfiah, who was leading the military incursion when and where the five Australian journalists had been murdered.

On November 12, thirty East Timorese and solidarity activists gathered outside the Indonesian Consulate in Darwin to mark the seventh anniversary of the Díli Massacre. We built a shrine to the dead with candles, a flood of plants and flowers with the centrepiece a traditional East Timorese sword resting on a shroud with the names of the dead woven into it. A huge East Timorese flag was carried along with signs demanding the release of political prisoners.

The liturgy was lead by Darwin-based East Timorese elder Veronica Miam who grieved, admonished the consulate and prayed in her traditional language. José Gusmão, whose two sons, brothers and father had been slain by the Indonesian military, led the protest. He spoke passionately about the suffering of his people.

We also reflected on Western complicity in, and non-violent resistance to, the genocide in East Timor. In the evening over eighty members of the East Timorese community gathered at a Darwin Catholic church for a mass remembering the dead. At the Santa Cruz cemetery in Díli over 10,000 East Timorese and foreign supporters gathered for the first public memorial of the 1991 massacre allowed by the Indonesian military. Only twelve months before, Hawks had flown low over Díli to scare off any public demonstrations.

## 3.3 *Ballot, Rhetoric and Reality*

As the new year of 1999 opened, the Australian Government leadership was doing back flips in relation to foreign policy on East Timor. After twenty-four years of bipartisan support for Indonesia's war on East Timor, Prime Minister Howard and Foreign Minister Downer announced that they now supported an act of self-determination by the people of East Timor. A few weeks later in January President Habibie announced that he would consider the possibility of a referendum in East Timor, a choice between independence and autonomy.

Over the next month international diplomacy between Indonesia and the UN produced an agreement for a ballot to be held for the East Timorese and commitments were made to working out the finer details with Portugal.

When I saw Bishop Belo in Brisbane, on the eve of my return to England at the end of February, he seemed very anxious and unhappy with the process. He had preferred a period, ten years at least, of autonomy, with a referendum vote as a conclusion. The general feeling however, was that this may be the only opportunity and should be seized no matter the consequences.

As international diplomacy abounded in the opening months of 1999, a parallel process was in motion on the ground in East Timor. The Indonesian military began to form pro-integration militias in each of East Timor's thirteen districts.

The integration-supporting militias had their roots in paramilitary organisations called partisans, established, organised and armed by the Indonesian military in 1978. For decades, these East Timorese guided Kopassus units into the hills on search-and-destroy missions against Fretilin guerrillas and independence sympathisers.

Initial finances for the militias came from a meeting between long-time collaborator, veteran pro Indonesian soldier (present at Balibo murders in 1975), intelligence figure and politician Thomas Gonçalves and Generals Adam Damiri, Kiki Shyanakri, Amirud and Minister for Transmigration Hendro Priyono.[6]

The reactivated militias were guaranteed finances, weapons and troop support if they defended the Indonesian flag in the coming period. Gonçalves was with Priyono when he told Governor Abilio's brother, Chiquito, the chief of the Transmigration Department in East Timor, to 'devote the whole departmental budget for the use of the militias.' Money was accessed from all departments, Transmigration, Agriculture and Forestry, as contributions to the 'socialisation of autonomy' project. This funded propaganda and militia activities to ensure the victory of the pro-Indonesian autonomy groups at the upcoming elections.

The intimate connection between ministries and militias was secured at a dinner at the Jakarta home of Indonesian Minister for Information, Yunus Yosfiah. Twenty-four years earlier Yunus had been in charge of the frontline unit in the initial invasion of East Timor. As noted, he has been accused of ordering the execution of Greg Shackleton, Brian Peters and the other journalists at Balibo.

Within a fortnight of the Jakarta meeting two million dollars arrived from Jakarta to launch the militias as a formal movement in every corner of East Timor. The money came through the FPDK (Forum for Unity, Democracy and Justice), a newly formed political front for the militias. Seventeen billion Rupiah was promised from Ali Alatas' Department of Foreign Affairs.

Nine billion was delivered by the Department's 'Special Envoy to East Timor'. Forced recruitment and murders began immediately. A distinguishing feature of the killings that occurred before the referendum was that nearly all the victims were mutilated as a gruesome message to others.

As Alatas began negotiating with the UN over the processes of the referendum, international attention was starting to focus on the growing terror campaign in East Timor. A direct connection with his department would have severely weakened Indonesia's bargaining position. The second instalment promised to the FPDK was cancelled. The momentum of the militias was picking up, but by March cash supply was slowing down. To ease the cash crisis the army provided militia leader Eurico Guterres with a suitcase of counterfeit bills, but the banks refused to accept them.

To permanently solve this liquidity problem, the leader of the FPDK from his government office in Díli cooked up a scheme with the Governor of East Timor and the cooperation of ministries in Jakarta, a scheme to plunder development and welfare funds that had been established to help the poor, a scheme where militia murderers could be put on the books as charity workers, financed largely by international donors, including the World Bank.

On March 26 1999, the Governor told Thomas Gonçalves, that from May 1, throughout the territory, the militia were to help liquidate all CNRT members, down to their grandchildren. If the people sought help from priests, nuns or the bishop, 'these too should be killed' After twenty-four years of being East Timor's most prominent integrationist, this was the limit for Gonçalves. He initially leaked information to independence leader Xanana Gusmão and then fled East Timor in April.

On April 6, there was an attack on Liquiça church where 2,000 refugees, many fleeing from the attack on Dato were taking refuge. This time, the attacking force consisted of soldiers from Battalion 142, from Kodim 1639, Liquiça police and Brimob troops as well as militia death squads lead by Eurico Guterres. Two priests were taken from the church to the local military command and, shortly after, the attack started.

Under the protection of the Brimob, troops surrounded the church and fired into the air. The militias started shooting into the church and a tear gas grenade was thrown in. The refugees taking sanctuary there scattered, trying to escape from the building. The scores of people trapped inside and outside the church were then set upon by men armed with knives, machetes and firearms and mercilessly stabbed, hacked and shot to death. The Liquiça massacre of fifty-seven dead, thirty-fiver wounded and fourteen missing sent a clear message that even the church was regarded as a legitimate target for the terror of the militias.

A few days later, a group of 120 people that had fled the countryside, where they had survived beatings, stabbings and rapes were targeted. They were taking refuge in a house in Díli when a large group of militiamen fuelled by drugs and money attacked. Dozens of refugees were shot and macheted as they scrambled to escape. Twelve of them died in the precincts of the house, the others were chased through the streets of Díli, fate unknown. Also in April 15 others were killed in other parts of East Timor. These killings were apparently done on credit against the expected arrival of World Bank funds. By May, the World Bank had advanced a general budget loan of $US500 million to the Indonesian Government, the second such loan in three months.

One of the first cheques drawn from the development fund at this time was for a million dollars. It was written directly to a government official, Radjarnka, who was able to cash the cheque or deposit directly to his personal account. Radjarkina was the Governor's secretary. He was also a senior member of the BRTT, one of the most prominent pro-integration groups. The cheque specifically stated that it was for the purposes of a 'Socialisation' team.

The World Bank became aware of the plan to use the money for the militia just weeks after finalising their US$500 million loan, but in effect did nothing. The cheques made out to individuals who were openly or covertly linked to the militias continued throughout May, June and July. Militia activity throughout the country picked up a momentum of intimidation and terror.

In May, an agreement was reached between the UN, Portugal and Indonesia for the ballot to be held in August. Most significantly the role of providing a safe and secure environment for this statement of self-determination was handed to the Indonesian military. In the event of a vote for independence the Indonesian military would continue to provide security through Phase Two until the vote had been ratified by Indonesian parliament. Only following ratification in Phase Three would an international force be introduced to secure transition to independence. This leap of logic that saw the same genocidal Indonesian military secure the role of objective arbitrator seemed to be non-negotiable and pregnant with disaster.

In England we could see the yawning gulf between the rhetoric and reality surrounding the referendum set for early August. By the beginning of June we had begun a vigil outside the Indonesian Embassy in Grosvenor Square, downtown London. A vigil had also begun outside the Indonesian Embassy in Washington DC. A weekly vigil and liturgy was initiated in Brisbane following the Liquiça massacre. On the July 17 anniversary of the annexation of East Timor by Indonesia we were joined by most East Timorese residents in Britain, coming in from Oxford, Liverpool, Newcastle, London and Birmingham. The UN had failed to provide a ballot venue in Britain, so most of the East Timorese were preparing to travel on to Portugal to register and vote.

Several countries, including Britain and Australia, sent unarmed policemen (Civpol) to act as peacekeepers and observers in the lead up to the referendum. A variety of Non-Government Organisations also sponsored observers. Terry Egan from the Liverpool Catholic Worker was accepted as an observer and left for East Timor in early August, the referendum having been postponed for three weeks by the UN due to a lack of security. Terry was stationed in the militia stronghold of Maliana, near the border of West Timor.

As Terry accompanied voters to the booths on referendum day (30 August 1999), we gathered for an all night vigil outside the London embassy.

Here we were a group of people who had been evangelised by Liverpool trial of the Ploughshares women and then by the East

Timorese survivors who had come to live with us, share their stories and show us how to resist. We set up a prayer position on the traffic island and rostered on for shifts as the rest of us vigilled opposite the Embassy. We passed the long night in the silent streets of this enormous city, surrounded by buildings of power and privilege. We meditated on an oppressed people half a world away risking their lives to cast a ballot. We reflected on how cities such as these wreak havoc on communities out of sight and out of mind. We prayed for a change of heart, a freedom from apathy and sedation and for the people finding courage while surrounded by guns, bullets and terror in East Timor.

## 3.4 *Scorched Earth Unleashed*

In all, 98.6% of the East Timorese who had registered turned out for the vote and the day passed without incident. As we left London and headed back to Liverpool, we shared an optimism that all may be well. We didn't have to wait long for reality to kick in and Bishop Belo's fears to be realised. As Belo had feared in February, a genocidal military doesn't all of a sudden embrace the expressed democratic will of a people. Within twenty-four hours of the conclusion of voting, days before an announcement of results were expected, the militias, under instruction from the Indonesian military, began making their move. At the village of Gleno, 150 UN staff were held in a ten hour siege. A UN helicopter was attacked by militia while attempting to pick up ballot boxes. UN staff at their largest centre in Díli were trapped by militia as refugees were chased into the compound. Shots were fired over the compound and a journalist was attacked.

As Terry Egan left from Díli airport, militia were picking people off their flights. Within two days militia had set up checkpoints and blockades at entry and exit points to Díli and strategic points around the town. Fires were being set and the trashing of houses, shops and buildings began in earnest. Announcement of the 78.5% vote for independence merely added fuel to an already ignited fire designed for a scorched earth objective.

Dozens of local UNAMET (UN Mission to East Timor) staffers were assassinated. A well-planned scorched earth policy was under way. General Wiranto responded to international criticism of TNI (The Indonesian Army) complicity with the militias by ordering another 1,400 troops into East Timor 'to restore order'. Within the week systematic forced deportations were under way.

US journalist Alan Nairn observed the Red Cross centre in Díli being trashed by militia, its occupants being lead away at gunpoint. He observed Indonesian police and soldiers disguised as militia looting, shooting and burning. He observed militia with free access to police centres where East Timorese were being forced to sign forms recanting their vote, issued with red and white headbands and loaded on trucks for deportation to West Timor. A reverse transmigration project was now under way that would see over 200,000 East Timorese ejected from their homeland within a few days. This was accompanied by an exodus of UN and foreign media. 4,000 people had sought refuge in the house of Bishop Belo and close to 2,000 at the UN compound.

By the end of the week the Australian Defence Minister admitted that two thirds of Díli had been destroyed in a systematic and organised fashion. Bishop Belo had sought refuge in Darwin and the Indonesian Justice Minister declared they would release and dump Xanana in the middle of a burning Díli. He was later given refuge at the British Embassy in Jakarta. By the end of the first week there had been an enormous exodus of foreign journalists and UN personnel. General Wiranto responded to further international criticism by declaring martial law in East Timor and asking the international community to give it 48 hours to work. After the performance of the TNI this seemed to be like throwing gasoline on the fire, but the Australian government agreed to this elastic deadline with Foreign Minister Downer saying 'I don't think we can be anything but sceptical, without wishing to be rude to the Indonesians, because they have 15,000 to 20,000 troops and armed police in East Timor and the place is just in a state of bloody chaos. What difference martial law is going to make, we'll just have to see.'

On Australian television (September 10 1999), Lieutenant-Colonel Bob Lowry (retired) of the Australian Defence Studies Centre, and former classmate of Wiranto, observed the method behind the madness.

'Well, the immediate objective is very clear. And that is to drive the UN out of East Timor, to discredit the UN process, with the reinforcement of troops being sent in there at the moment, to launch another operation against Falantil. And as well as that, of course, by the devastation they've wrought on East Timor to make sure the rest of Indonesia knows that the military will not tolerate any move towards secession.' He also made the observation. 'The Indonesian military are constituted for internal security primarily, and they've got a limited conventional war capacity.'[7]

Securing what for who against who was not explored by the good Lieutenant-Colonel. On this program it was also revealed that the Australian Defence Signals Directorate had recorded phone conversations between an Indonesian colonel and militia groups planning a post-election rampage.

The fact that the Australian Defence Signals Directorate were listening in on all radio and telephone conversations in East Timor throughout the year gives the lie to the year-long fiction that the Australian Government believed the militias were independent from the Indonesian military and Government, a fiction promoted heavily by the Australian Government's Department of Foreign Affairs and Trade. The Australian Government knew all along that militias could not have existed without the organisation, funding and arming of the Indonesian Government and military. Even at this late stage, Downer's remark to wait and see what martial law was to produce was a desperate attempt to keep this fiction alive. This fiction not only cost the lives of thousands of East Timorese but possibly also led to the suicide of Merv Jenkins, the senior Australian military liaison officer to the United States.

It has been standard practice for decades for the senior military officer at the Australian embassy in Washington DC to hand over carte blanche Australian military intelligence to the

United States.

In return, Australia receives a certain amount of relevant intelligence gathered by US satellites, room under the nuclear umbrella etc.

During the lead up to the East Timor ballot, Merv Jenkins handed on, as was standard practice, Australian gathered intelligence received at the DC Embassy to the Pentagon. However, this intelligence increasingly included information on how the Indonesian military were establishing and financing pro-integration militia death squads in East Timor. This was information that Australian Foreign affairs bureaucrats wished to keep hidden from the US. They were desperate to sustain the fiction of militia autonomy. The US backed strategy to replace the corrupt inefficient generals with a new ruling class of more IMF obedient technocrats had left the Australian Foreign Affairs establishment behind. The Australian bureaucrats remained loyal to the generals, as they had remained loyal to Soeharto, trying to cover up Indonesian activities in the lead up to the UN ballot in East Timor. Discovering that such revealing information was being handed to the US, the bureaucrats accused Merv Jenkins of betraying his country.[8]

In the last months of his life Merv Jenkins was caught in an historic crossroads between the Australian establishment's fifty-year subservience to US military power and a thirty-year loyalty to the Indonesian generals. He took the accusations of betrayal seriously, writing a letter about loyalty and honour and then hanging himself in the garage of his Arlington, Virginia residence. His family demanded a public inquiry into his death that would expose how much the Australian Government knew and when. The Australian Government tried to keep the inquiry in-house to sustain their latest fiction.

For the next three weeks the beast we had fed for thirty years rampaged, burned and slaughtered across East Timor and the television screens and front pages of Australia, Britain and the US. The use of militias as a front in the systematic execution of dissidents, rape of women and children, forced deportation and terror of the civilian population by the Indonesian military was

92

nothing new.

It echoed the October-December 1965 period as Soeharto's paratroopers secured the coup sweeping through Central Java heading to East Java and Northern Sumatra and onto Bali leaving over half a million dead in their wake. The killing was on such a huge scale as to raise a sanitation problem in East Java and Northern Sumatra, where the smell of decaying flesh was pervasive and rivers were impassable because of the clogging of human bodies. It had been systematically repeated since the invasion of 1975 with paratroopers and militia throughout the villages and mountains of East Timor costing over 200,000 East Timorese lives.

The qualitative difference this time was that it was exposed in the mainstream media, from the gruesome decapitations and systematic destruction, to the arrogance of the granny-killing, karaoke-singing, smirking Generals who believed themselves untouchable even as they lorded it over a crippled economy while attacking a UN mission.

In London, accompanied by the monks of Nipponzon Myohoji we returned to maintain daily eight hour vigils outside the Indonesian Embassy. We were occasionally joined by larger mobilisations such as 'Campaign Against the Arms Trade' and 'Amnesty International'. The Portuguese community organised a weekend rally outside 10 Downing St. As the massacres got worse it was a struggle to maintain a non-violent discipline in the face of the arrogance and cynicism of embassy staff. This led to a number of confrontations with staff, ranging form weeping and begging to stop the violence to blocking the Ambassador's limousine. We were dealt with by the permanent police guard placed on the embassy and by rapidly deployed vans of riot police. On the whole, the police were relatively sympathetic and aware that the British police were presently in the Díli UN compound being fired on by militia and Indonesian soldiers.

In Brisbane, during the first week of militia violence, several hundred people gathered outside the Department of Foreign Affairs and Trade building with fourteen people carrying out a day long occupation of offices.

The protest demanded asylum for East Timorese, an end to the training of Indonesian troops, sanctions imposed on Indonesia and a freezing of World Bank/IMF loans. It ended with police using force to evict protesters.

Trade Unions began blacklisting Indonesian shipping and flights around the country. At Sydney, Melbourne and Adelaide airports, trade unionists and East Timorese blockaded Garuda flights to Indonesia calling for a boycott. In Brisbane four women were arrested during a citizens' closure of Garuda's offices. This was followed by over 1,000 people demonstrating outside the office, with one trade unionist arrested after throwing an egg at the office.

## 3.5 *Forgetting as a Means of Managing Dissent*

On September 10, Lisa Bridle, Jim Dowling, Rachel Harrison and Kerry Kreevy of 'Brisbane Faith and Resistance' entered the Department of Foreign Affairs and Trade building to carry out an exorcism of a department that had claimed the lives of Merv Jenkins and untold East Timorese.

Jim Dowling wrote on the office wall in blood 'God Forgive Us!' while the group carried out a rite of exorcism. Their statement declared,

'The Department of Foreign Affairs and Trade is directly implicated in the current genocide which is occurring in East Timor. Successive Australian Governments since 1975 have endorsed the slaughter and brutal repression of the East Timorese people.

Our Government callously recognised Indonesian sovereignty thus sanctioning the terror of the invasion and the continuing oppression.

We trained the murderous Indonesian military despite evidence of rampant human rights abuses in East Timor and elsewhere.

We agreed to share with Indonesia the spoils of its bloody war on East Timor in order to rob the Timorese of their oil in the Timor Gap.

This disgraceful disregard for the most basic human

rights of the people of East Timor has occurred because this Department has advised the government that such 'policies' are in Australia's best economic and security interests. These policies, particularly the Defence Co-operation Pact with Indonesia and military aid are a potent reminder of our cowardly betrayal of the East Timorese who lost their lives protecting Australian soldiers in WWII. Our courting of Indonesia has ultimately led us to the present situation of an Indonesian military regime which quite reasonably feels immune from international scrutiny. As apologists for the Indonesian military dictatorship, we have proven time and time again that any rhetoric of human rights is easily abandoned for our perceived economic gain.

So we come today to these offices to name, bind and cast out the evil spirits which have guided our Department of Foreign Affairs and Trade. At this time of immense suffering for the people of East Timor, we choose not to be ruled by hopelessness and despair. Instead we act because we trust in a God of hope and love, a God who is more powerful than the forces of evil and death.

We seek to dispel the spirit of apathy which has tempted us with riches and comfort and hardened our hearts to the cries of God's people. We come to reject the spirits of greed and violence which have left this Department silent and indifferent to the deliberate crushing of the East Timorese people. We act in a spirit of humility, knowing that we too have failed our brothers and sisters in East Timor. We act in obedience and faith knowing that the demons are impotent in the presence of the transforming love of Jesus Christ.

We implore the Australian Government to immediately
   · Cancel the Defence Co-operation Pact with Indonesia
   · Rescind the Timor Gap Treaty
   · Cease all economic and military aid

· Confiscate the Indonesian Generals assets
· Close all Indonesian Embassies.'
All four were arrested and charged with criminal damage. Jim Dowling was held in custody for three weeks on warrants arising from previous non-violent resistance. He immediately went on a fast in repentance for Australian betrayal of the East Timorese.

In Díli, the UN had ordered the evacuation of its personnel from its remaining compound, in effect to abandon the 1,000 East Timorese who had scaled the barbed wire to find refuge with them. In a most courageous act, eighty rank and file UN personnel, police, activists, journalists and observers refused the order to evacuate in order to protect the East Timorese. *Sunday Times* correspondent Marie Colvin reported on September 10, 1999:

> 'Well it's deteriorated rapidly today shortly after a convoy left evacuating UN staff, local staff and a number of journalists...most of the soldiers, Indonesian soldiers around the perimeter went to the convoy to secure it. Militia immediately poured against the walls of the UN compound threatening to throw grenades over the walls, panicked the refugees who were outside so much so that two little women threw themselves on to the barbed wire over the walls. They're badly injured. Then they started demanding cars and vehicles and were joined by the army in smashing up windshields to get into those cars. I saw these two militia trying to smash in the windshield of a pickup truck. They were for some reason, unable to do so and several soldiers came along and managed to smash it with their rifle butts at which point the mixed group of militia and military started looting the vehicle and trying to get it started. I don't think you need much more of an example to say that they are cooperating.
>
> There are thousands of refugees inside the compound. They're very scared. They're targets of these people. They think they're going to be slaughtered. They have experience, they're probably right.
>
> What's keeping them from panicking is the fact that

80 members of the UN staff have volunteered to stay behind. You have to remember, these refugees are in this position because they voted for independence. One of the slogans-the UN monitored that election-one of the slogans was 'Don't be afraid, the UN will stay.' People then voted and are now targets. Anyone who voted for independence-which is as we know 80% of the population - is being targeted by the militia.'[9]

Some East Timorese took their chances and attempted an escape into the mountains behind the compound at night. They were accompanied by Max Stahl, who took night vision footage and managed to get it out of the country. As all Westerners were finally evacuated along with the East Timorese in the compound, Max stayed on taking for the hills. It was in the hills where the second wave of death would hit hardest in the form of starvation, disease and dehydration.

In Australia a mass movement in response to the massacres in East Timor arose rapidly, with demonstrations of over 25,000 people in both Sydney and Melbourne. Unfortunately this movement was media generated and quickly controlled by the Labor and Liberal Parties. These parties had lead successive Australian Governments delivering twenty-four years of policies to oppress the East Timorese and support the Indonesian war effort.

These parties that had lead the only governments in the world to recognise the legitimacy of the Indonesian invasion, were both going in to overdrive in terms of damage control. The ALP managed to impose leadership on the movement and downsize the demands concerning the East Timor crisis to one of Australian military intervention. The voices of long-time East Timor solidarity were effectively silenced or marginalised at such events. At a packed Brisbane City Hall rally hosted by the Labor Mayor, the speaking platform was dominated by Labor hacks, church bureaucrats, and assorted opportunists who, at best, had maintained their silence through the twenty-four year war against the people of East Timor.

The Labor Party controlled movement made the demand for

military intervention and the Liberal Party Government met it. They had been preparing an extra brigade of soldiers for this very contingency since the beginning of the year.

After several weeks of international pressure, forced deportation of over 200,000 East Timorese and a successful scorched earth policy enacted, President Habibie relented to the request to allow international forces in to restore order.

As quickly as the mass movement of concern for East Timor was turned on by the mainstream media in Australia, it was turned off. The mechanism of safety valve expressions of concern, reassurance of 'we've heard your message' from the powers that be and a return to 'passivity while the powerful get on with their own agendas' was repeated once again.

The agendas came thick and fast. The post-Vietnam military priority was to proceed with minimum Australian casualties as the priority and secondly to salvage relationships with the Indonesian Government and military and somewhere down the line display a concern for the East Timorese. Independence for East Timor and confronting our support for the genocidal Indonesian military were not on the agenda. It's instructive to remember that the only long time demands of the East Timor solidarity movement that were met, namely the suspension of military ties and the scrapping of the Oil Treaty, were 'granted' by the Indonesian Government, not the Australian Government.

The Indonesian military, laden with all the loot they could carry, left East Timor for the West where they had secured 200,000 East Timorese hostages and where their militia had free access to the camps. The Australians accepted a process where the refugees would be asked if they wished to return and were expected to answer in the presence of armed militia.

The UN Human Rights investigation into war crimes carried out by the Indonesian military in this period was waived for guarantees that the Indonesians would investigate themselves. The Indonesian military continued (and continue) to bankroll the militia in a contra type harassment on the border.

Such 'bushfires' from Aceh to Ambon strengthens the

internal political power of the Indonesian military in their power struggle with the technocrats and other pretenders in the post-Soeharto era. The assortment of economic opportunists and carpetbaggers assembled by the Australian Government to reap from the rebuilding of East Timor was breathtaking in its gymnastic opportunism. Many of these people had profited from twenty-four years of Indonesian destructive occupation and were now discovering that there was UN and World Bank money to be milked in East Timor's reconstruction.

Media generated sentiment in Australia was rapidly transferred from the East Timorese to 'our courageous diggers' in the most successful rehabilitation of the Australian armed forces in the post-Vietnam War era. This reached a pre-Christmas crescendo with the live telecast of the 'Tour of Duty' concert for the troops live from Díli initiated by Vietnam Veteran Doc Neesen, headlined by Kylie Minogue and John Farnham and addressed by General Cosgrove. This was the most watched televised event of the year in Australia. There was no space for an East Timorese voice at this event. The canonisation of Cosgrove, a refreshing personality in contrast to the arrogance of the Indonesian Generals, proceeded at pace. This unrepentant Vietnam warrior acknowledged his good relations with the Indonesian military as key to minimal Australian casualties. He has since been fast tracked to head the Australian military.

This transfer of sentiment was complete by March 2000. The Australian Government was able to pull off the forced return of the East Timorese refugees they had reluctantly evacuated from the UN compound siege, on the same day as welcoming home the first rotation of troops with a triumphalist parade through the streets of Sydney. They were returning these East Timorese to a country with little infrastructure or shelter in the middle of monsoon season when food was scarce and disease was rampant.

Those of us who hoped that the 'East Timor Crisis' would provide a catharsis for the Australian nation to look at our sins of military, economic, diplomatic exploitation of our neighbours, a time of repentance and resistance, were to be disappointed.

Instead of sharing the post-WWII German experience of having to stare into the ovens and confront our complicity in genocide, we experienced a manufactured elevation of Australian involvement in East Timor as a high point of national pride. It was a process amazing to behold, which could only be possible in a culture of popular amnesia, a process that would ensure the same policies of the twenty-four year war in East Timor could be repeated in West Papua and elsewhere.

This process climaxed in kitsch at the annual Logies (Australia's television awards) where General Cosgrove was the guest of honour. An award for East Timorese coverage was given to Channel Seven, a slap in the face for the journalists of ABC and SBS who had for at least the previous decade tried to cover the war on East Timor with limited resources. As the Channel Seven reporter accepted the award he made no mention of Channel Seven employees Greg Shackleton, Gary Cunningham or Tony Stewart or their Channel Nine colleagues Brian Peters and Malcolm Rennie who were slain in the invasion of East Timor, and no mention of the cost of their journalism or the cover-up of their murders.

# 3.6 A Subversive Memory for a Prophetic Community

I remember sitting next to Malcolm Rennie's mother as she watched video footage of her sons last day of life, hearing an uncontrollable gasp of grief.

I remember speaking to Malcolm Rennie's cousin surrounded by riot police, before sprinting across the road into London's Mayfair Continental Hotel where four of us dressed as the slain journalists attempted to gatecrash the Indonesian ambassadors lunch and press conference. It was a day his government was denying food drops to the starving East Timorese survivors in the mountains.

I remember being with Brian Peter's sister outside the Indonesian Embassy in London as she demanded justice through the intercom.

I remember watching Greg Shackleton's widow confront the Australian trainers of Indonesian troops at the Canungra Land Warfare Centre.

I remember sharing a Liverpool cell with Kupa after he had been denied sanctuary by my government during an occupation of the Australian Embassy in Jakarta.

I remember welcoming an anxious Rui into our community months after he had been tortured by Indonesian military and watch him depart a year later healthy and strong.

I remember dancing to Afonso's Brisbane band and

watching him perform traditional dances in a local park. He had been twenty years in exile.

I remember the Indonesian ambassador writhing in anger in the back seat as I knelt in front of his limo.

I remember the unapologetic arrogance of Evans as we gate crashed his barbie.

I remember being in the courtroom as the Liverpool jury concluded that the crime was with British Aerospace, not with the four women prisoners who had disarmed the Hawk.

I remember an East Timorese defendant asking a BAe employee in the broken English of cross-examination 'Why do you want to kill?'

I remember that four days before Robin Cook announced a suspension of weapon sales to Indonesia there were four Hawks with Indonesian markings at BAe Warton. Two days before the announcement only one remained. The day after, three were in Thailand en route to Indonesia. The suspension lasted all of three months.

I remember many vigils outside embassies, courts, and corporate offices.

I remember many powerful people saying they were powerless.

I remember many refugees made to feel quite at home.

I remember a lot of celebration: liturgical, musical, cross-cultural, cross-generational, a lot of solidarity and spontaneity.

I remember a lot of First World folks shaken and awakened, opening scripture together, breaking bread, sharing wine, reaching out, taking risks, jumping fences, blocking doors, speaking out, sitting in, offering hospitality and accepting it.

It may be true that military, media, corporations and governments are flexing their power and claiming the process of defining reality for East Timor, while putting us in the First World back to sleep with the reassurance to leave everything to unrepentant politicians, arms industry magnates, military leaders, the World Bank bureaucrats and the 'international ambulance chasers' of aid bureaucracies.

But that's not the end of the story.

There are always two stories.

As a friend says, there is 'history written from above and history written from below.'

As it is for East Timor, so it is for us. As Woody Guthrie would say, 'The secret to life is showing up!' or as in Acts of the Apostles, 'hanging in together.'

So we re-gather, break open the Scripture, share the bread and wine, reflect, wrestle the temptations of co-option to manage the poor or manage dissent, to embrace power, wealth and status.

Instead we attempt to embrace the kingdom of precariousness and solidarity and pray to be delivered from our deafness to the cries of the poor, blindness to the arrangements that bring us privilege as we exploit others, and the gift of courage to speak truth to power.

# Endnotes

[1] Ched Meyers *Who Will Roll Away the Stone?* Orbis Press, Maryknoll, New York, 1994

[2] Bill Kellerman 'The Hospitality of God' *Sojourners Magazine*

[3] Wes Howard Brooks *Becoming Children of God* Orbis Press, Maryknoll, New York 1994

[4] John Pilger *Hidden Agendas* Vintage, London 1998

[5] Noam Chomsky *The Washington Connection and Third World Fascism* South End Press, Boston 1979

[6] *Dateline* February 16 2000 Report SBS Television, Australia

[7] *7.30 Report* September 10 1999, ABC Television, Australia

[8] *Four Corners* February 2000, ABC Television, Australia

[9] *7.30 Report* September 10 1999, ABC Television, Australia